W9-AYB-907

BOOK ONE
Second Edition

Catechists in Formation

Introduction to Catechetical Methods

Written by
Peter Ries

Consultant
David Riley

Benziger Publishing Company
Mission Hills, California

Photo Credits
Daemmrich/Tony Stone Worldwide 2-12; Mary Kate Denny/Photo Edit 4-15; Nicholas Devore/Tony Stone Worldwide 1-7; Myrleen Ferguson/Photo Edit 2-4, 2-16, 4-8, 9-15; Barbara Filet/Tony Stone Worldwide 9-13; David R. Frazier/Tony Stone Worldwide 6-5; Tony Freeman/Photo Edit 2-3, 3-11, 7-2, 8-13; 8-15; Jeff Greenberg/Photo Edit 5-9, 7-16; Howard Grey/Tony Stone Worldwide Richard Hutchins/Photo Edit 7-8; McCarter/Photo Edit 4-3; Michael Newman/Photo Edit 2-6; Jim Pickerell/Tony Stone Worldwide 1-13; Ken Rogers/Westlight 7-10; Loren Santow/Tony Stone Worldwide 2-10; Rhoda Sidney/Photo Edit 4-14; Donald Smetzer/Tony Stone Worldwide 2-11; Superstock 1-2, 1-5, 1-6, 1-8, 1-11, 1-12, 2-7, 2-9, 3-2, 3-4, 3-7, 3-8, 3-12, 3-14, 3-15, 4-7, 4-10, 4-13, 5-2, 5-3, 5-15, 6-3, 6-7, 6-11, 6-14, 7-4, 7-9, 7-12, 7-13, 8-2, 8-6, 8-8, 8-10, 8-16, 9-2, 9-7, 9-9, 9-10; Tony Stone Worldwide 9-16; Brian Vikander/Westlight 7-14; Lee White/Westlight 1-10; David Young-Wolff Photo Edit 2-15, 4-4, 5-13

Book One Table of Contents

Introduction .... *iv*

Chapter 1 The Role of the Catechist 1-1

Chapter 2 Understanding How Faith Develops 2-1

Chapter 3 Knowing Your Students 3-1

Chapter 4 Responding to Your Students as Persons 4-1

Chapter 5 Connecting Learning and Teaching 5-1

Chapter 6 A Process for Planning Lessons 6-1

Chapter 7 Effective Teaching Techniques 7-1

Chapter 8 Dealing with Discipline 8-1

Chapter 9 Succeeding as a Catechist 9-1

Book One Introduction

Welcome to Benziger's *Catechists in Formation*, a complete introductory training program for catechists. Through the use of a four-part educational process, you will come to know the information, attitudes, and skills you need to be an effective catechist.

Catechists in Formation was designed to be used effectively in many types of religious education training programs. This Introduction will describe the program's philosophy and the content of its various books. You will be given several options for using this program and suggestions for implementing it under the model you choose.

Audience

Catechists in Formation was written for the benefit of any man or woman engaged in the passing on of the Catholic faith, whether that person is a full-time, paid, professional teacher in a Catholic school setting or a first time, volunteer teacher in a parish school of religion. Because of its unique design, each level of teacher can take from *Catechists in Formation* what he or she needs in order to improve his or her catechetical skills and theological knowledge.

Professional educators, proficient in educational method, might use *Book One*, "Introduction to Catechetical Methods," as a brief review or refresher course. Even the most experienced educator will find here valuable suggestions for teaching a particular age group or intended outcome. *Book Two*, "Introduction to Theological Studies," would then be used to update teachers in the teachings of the Catholic faith, as well as demonstrate for them effective methods of communicating that faith to their students.

Volunteer teachers will want to pay special attention to *Book One*, using it as a workbook to develop the teaching skills they need in order to become a more effective catechist. Once they become comfortable using effective teaching methods, volunteer teachers can turn their attention to *Book Two* and learn what the Church believes and practice teaching methods to effectively hand that faith on to the next generation of believers.

Throughout both books, "Introduction to Catechetical Methods" and "Introduction to Theological Studies," the term "catechist" is used to mean both the professional and the volunteer teacher. *Sharing the Life of Faith* describes teachers and principals in Catholic schools, as well as parish catechists, parish coordinators, and Directors of Religious Education as catechists. Although their roles are different, both the professional and the volunteer teacher are vital to the students' growth into a mature, conscious, and active faith, and thus deserve the title of catechist.

Philosophy of the Program

Catechists in Formation builds upon the National Catechetical Directory, *Sharing the Light of Faith* and the *Catechism of the Catholic Church*. There are eight basic assumptions integral to the philosophy of the program:

1. Religious education is more than the handing on of religious truths. Its goal is growth in faith, which implies both formation and transformation, leading one to live out the Gospel as part of a believing community.

2. Religious education is a lifelong process. Everyone, including catechists, is always a learner and is always growing in faith.

3. The role of catechist is central to the life of the Church. Systematic growth in faith is fostered through this ministry.

4. Adequate preparation and formation are indispensable for every catechist.

   "The response to this call [to be a catechist] includes willingness to give time and talent, not only to catechizing others, but to one's own continued growth in faith and understanding" Sharing the Light of Faith, #206.

   Good will alone does not ensure success. A living, active faith does not necessarily include the basic skills necessary to be a catechist. Volunteers as well as professional teachers need catechist formation.

5. Each local parish must determine its own approach to catechist formation by assessing and providing for the catechists' needs.

6. It is appropriate to promote and expect formation for all catechists because (a) the role of catechist

requires specific skills and attitudes, (b) catechists are central to the life of the Church, and (c) catechists themselves expect assistance.

7. Among the many possible approaches to promoting growth in faith, **experiential religious education** is of considerable value.

> *"Catechists should encourage people to reflect on their significant experiences and respond to God's presence there. Sometimes they will provide appropriate experiences. They should seek to teach the whole person, using both cognitive (intellectual) and affective (emotional) techniques"* Sharing the Light of Faith, #176.

Catechists in Formation reflects this experiential approach to religious education.

8. Sound religious education stresses the need to adapt the teaching and learning processes to the needs of the times and to the age levels of the people involved.

The Components of the Program

◄ There are three components to the program, *Catechists in Formation*:

- **Book One: "Introduction to Catechetical Methods"**
- **Book Two: "Introduction to Theological Studies"**
- The **Program Manual**

In addition, each chapter of *Book One* and *Book Two* may be ordered individually, separate from the books. This allows each parish to easily pick and choose the topics it wishes to teach and gives it an option on how the materials are presented to the teachers.

Each of the titles are designed to be used by the catechist as a workbook and journal. The catechist will use the books as their personal trainer in which they write notes, develop program ideas, and practice techniques to which they will frequently return. This introduction will describe *Book One* and *Book Two* in detail and will sketch out the contents of the Program Manual.

Elements in Book One and Book Two

Book One, "Introduction to Catechetical Methods," contains nine topics, all aimed at helping the catechist understand and apply the technical aspects of teaching religion, classroom management, and faith development.

Book Two, "Introduction to Theological Studies," contains twelve chapters focusing on the basic theological content required by most diocesan religious education guidelines.

Each chapter of *Catechists in Formation* is divided into four parts—**Experience, Message, Discovery,** and **Response**—that make up the catechetical process used in most modern religious education textbook series. Too often, catechists are taught using methods appropriate for the college classroom, but inappropriate for their students. In modeling the process by which catechists are to teach, *Catechists in Formation* better prepares the teacher to meet the needs of the students.

Each chapter begins with an introductory quote and a series of student **learning outcomes.** From there, it moves quickly into the heart of the material.

- **Part I: Experience** The process of catechesis always involves sharing the stories of the Catholic faith following Jesus' example. Since the publication of *Christian Religious Education* by Dr. Thomas Groome, religious educators have recognized the importance, once again, of following Jesus' method.

  Part I contains realistic stories, directed toward the topic of discussion in the chapter, that are meant to capture the catechists' attention and touch upon their experience. In this way, they are prepared to work with the material presented in Part II.

- **Part II: Message** It is here that the students are introduced directly to the topic in practical, clear, and readable prose. The basic points of content are introduced here.

- **Part III: Discovery** The content of the lesson is further developed here, with the catechist actually working with the material and applying it to his or her teaching or learning situation.

- **Part IV: Response** The final part of the catechetical process is always a response to the message. Here, catechists use exercises and prayer to help them develop the skills presented in the lesson or determine how they will use what they've learned with their students.

Spread throughout *Catechists in Formation* are features, activities, and exercises. Of particular note are:

- **Pause a Moment . . .** These are questions for writing and discussion that follow most major heads.

- **The New Commandment** This feature highlights quotations from the New Testament appropriate to the topic being discussed.

- **The Church Teaches**   This feature introduces catechists to Church teaching as presented in the *Catechism of the Catholic Church*.

Each chapter ends with a prayer activity and a bibliography.

Because *Catechists in Formation* is designed to be used as a personal workbook by the catechist, writing rules are provided frequently to facilitate note-taking.

- **Memo**   This feature asks the catechist to consider a question and provides a convenient space for the catechist's answer.

- **Activities**   Many of the features in *Catechists in Formation* are actual worksheets for the catechist to use. Depending on the exercise involved, writing rules or a boxed space are provided so that the activity can be easily completed.

- **Notes**   In many of the side margins, a "notepad" is provided to encourage the catechists' personal response to the questions raised in the narrative. **Notes** appears most frequently alongside the feature, **Pause a Moment.**

Elements of the Program Manual

A Program Manual is available for use with *Catechists in Formation*. Detailed approaches for teaching each lesson are presented in the "Lesson Guides." Lesson Guides for *Book One* and *Book Two* are combined in the one Program Manual.

The Lesson Guides can be used effectively in both non-directed and directed group studies. Diocesan formation programs will also find these lesson guides are correlated to catechetical guidelines.

Options for Using the Program

There are three basic models for using *Catechists in Formation*: (1) self-study, (2) non-directed group study, and (3) directed group study.

Self-Study

In places where there is no director of religious education or very little opportunity for a formal program, *Catechists in Formation* provides an option for structured self-study. Professional teachers or volunteer catechists can use this program for personal or professional enrichment. The following list offers a step-by-step plan for using this program for self-study.

1. Plan your schedule. Although the two books are ordered in a logical, developmental sequence, each chapter is self-contained, and may be used when you need it. You decide what and when you will study.

2. Choose a quiet place to complete your reading, reflecting, and activities. The best material in the world is useless unless you take the time to study it, make it your own, and then decide how you can use it.

3. Share what you have learned with other catechists and apply your knowledge to your teaching. Discuss what you've learned with others so that you can clarify what you've discovered and can collectively support each others' efforts.

Nondirected Group-Study

When the full benefit of using *Catechists in Formation* in a group setting is desired, but someone to direct the program is lacking, a nondirected group study approach can be used.

1. **Conduct a needs and interest survey** to determine which of the twenty-one topics in the two books are most relevant for your use. (Remember, you can order copies of just those chapters that you plan to study.) If there are many new volunteer catechists in the group, it is recommended that you begin with the topics in *Book One*, "Introduction to Catechetical Methods."

2. **Plan your calendar.** Consider how long the program will run (have definite beginning and ending dates), and which days you will meet. Determine how many topics you want to cover in the duration of the program.

3. **Consider how long you want each meeting to last.** The length of your meetings affects the way you organize the session. With group discussion and the sharing of answers, there is enough material in each topic to last a full two and one-half hours. For shorter meetings, adjustments will have to be made. Consult the Learning Guides suggested in the Program Manual to adjust your meeting plan; however, a short guide is presented here.

> - **One and one-half hour meetings:** Have the catechists read the material and complete the exercises at home during the week prior to the meeting. Use your time together to share answers and practice techniques.

- **Two-hour meetings:** Have the participants read **Part I: Experience** and complete the exercise found there at home. During the meeting, the catechists can read and discuss the remaining material together. Choose only a few of the many activities to complete together, concentrating on those in **Part IV: Response.** Allow for a 15-minute break in addition to the two hours of study.

4. If needed to harmonize schedules and choices of topics, consider forming a second group with its own agenda and schedule.

5. Order the books (or individual chapters) six to eight weeks in advance to allow time for shipment. If you wish to begin in September, order your books in May or June. The materials you order will be determined by the topics your group has chosen to study.

   Remember, unauthorized duplication of Book One or Book Two (or any of the individual chapters) is a violation of copyright law.

6. Decide where to hold the session. Groups can meet on the parish premises, in faculty rooms, or in individuals' homes. If the groups are to meet on the parish premises, schedule the program on the parish calendar early in the year.

7. Appoint a facilitator (an individual, a couple, or a team of two) to chair each meeting. Group participants can take turns (see "The Facilitator's Responsibilities" at the right).

8. Appoint a group coordinator to oversee the organizational details, including handling registrations and ordering the books.

The Group Coordinator's Role

The role of group coordinator involves organizing the behind-the-scenes details so that the group meetings run smoothly. This list tells the responsibilities of the group coordinator.

1. Arrange for the registration of all participants and collect any necessary fees.

2. Order the materials. (See #5 under "Nondirected Group Study.")

3. Prepare for the first meeting. The first meeting, whether in a home or in the parish, is important. Inform the participants that the first meeting will last 15 minutes longer than future meetings. This will allow time for organizational details to be handled.

4. Organize the small groups before the first session and ask one person in each group to act as discussion leader. Recall these points as you form the groups.
   - Small groups should consist of no fewer than five and no more than ten.
   - A mixture of ages affords all a more extensive learning experience.
   - Groups should not be made up solely of catechists who teach at the same level.
   - Husbands and wives benefit from being in different groups.
   - Small groups should, if possible, contain a variety of socioeconomic, and ethnic backgrounds, as well as a mixture of single and married people.

5. Prepare the meeting place so that it is comfortable. Have plenty of moveable chairs. Each small group should be given an area large enough so as not to interfere with other small groups. Make sure the space matches the size of the group. A large hall is not appropriate for one or two small groups. Good ventilation and proper temperature are important. Discourage smoking during the meeting.

6. Have all supplies on hand for each meeting: name tags, pencils, extra copies of *Catechists in Formation,* and refreshments.

The Facilitator's Responsibilities

The role of the facilitator is to see that the meeting runs smoothly. A facilitator is neither the leader nor the teacher. Any adult who is enthusiastic about the program and who is willing to prepare for the meeting can facilitate. The facilitator's responsibilities include:

1. Prepare for the meeting. Read the material, complete the activities, and be prepared for discussion.

2. Keep track of time, and move the group along so that you can finish the session on time. Keep the group informed on the amount of time remaining in the session.

3. Participate in a small group or in the overall group as an equal member. Do not take the position of teacher. You may, however, act as discussion leader in a small group.

4. Refer to the Lesson Guides in the Program Manual for step-by-step instructions for facilitating each lesson. Follow the topic page by page in the order presented unless there is good reason for not doing so. The following suggestions can help move the group through the process smoothly:

- Have the group read the material either (a) before the session, (b) during the session quietly, (c) aloud in a large group, or (d) aloud in small groups. Ask the group how they would like to cover the material.

- If you decide to do any part of the material at home prior to the session, adjust the time schedule to allow for group discussion of that material.

- Allow participants to ask any questions as they read. Do not attempt to answer those questions yourself, but encourage the group to search for answers together. Keep a watch on time and don't allow these activities to drag on.

- Allow plenty of time for participants to share their responses to the activities. Encourage discussion of people's responses, but accept no criticism of someone's answers.

- End the meeting on time. If you haven't finished a topic or a section, ask the group if they want to finish where they left off at the next meeting, or complete the rest at home privately. Leave room at the next meeting for comments on the work studied at home.

- Begin and end each session with prayer. Invite different participants to prepare a brief prayer to begin each meeting. End the meeting with the "Prayer Response" at the end of each chapter.

- When a topic is finished, provide the group with an evaluation from the Program Manual.

Directed Group Study

The main difference between nondirected group study and directed group study is the Catechist Trainer. A Catechist Trainer is a professional religious educator—religious or lay—who assumes the responsibilities assigned to the group coordinator and the facilitator and who assumes the role of teacher.

Suggestions for the Catechist Trainer

The following will help the Catechist Trainer use *Catechists in Formation* most effectively.

1. Use the Program Manual as your guide throughout the planning and implementation of the program.

2. Assess the needs of the group before setting a schedule.

3. Clarify what the program is intended to accomplish.

4. Based upon the needs of your students, determine the number and order of the topics to be covered. A detailed method is in the Manual.

5. Design publicity for the program to ensure a good registration.

6. Be prepared to supplement the material presented in **Part II: Message and Part III: Discovery.** Use the teaching suggestions found in the Manual as a guide.

7. Use various teaching techniques to promote understanding of the content and to make your presentations more dynamic. Refer to the Manual for suggestions on appropriate techniques to use.

8. Decide how you will use the writing and discussion activities throughout each session. You might want to have participants work through the material on their own prior to the sessions.

9. Have students monitor their progress by using the evaluation form that you can reproduce from the Program Manual.

Scheduling the Program

One attractive feature about *Catechists in Formation* is its flexibility. If the individual chapters are purchased, you can arrange the topics in any order you choose. Of course, each book is self-contained and may be followed exactly in the order given, which is a logical presentation of the topics.

The following list offers optional ways of scheduling the program:

1. One topic a week for twenty-one weeks. Or do the same for shorter programs of three, four, or six weeks.

2. A one-day seminar for faculty members.

3. One topic at monthly catechist meetings or grade level planning sessions.

4. A week-long summer program.

5. An in-service program for the catechists of the Catholic school.

6. In cooperation with another parish or parishes. Share each others' resources, discussion leaders, and Catechist Trainers.

Benziger

The Role of the Catechist

A catechist is faith, hope, and love attached to arms and legs, aches and pains, family duties and not enough time.

A catechist is an ordinary person who is extraordinary because he or she teaches as Jesus did.

A catechist is faithful to the past, open to the future, but especially dedicated to deepening the faith of the present generation.

From the poem, "A Catechist Is"
by Monsignor John Francis Murphy

BOOK ONE

In this chapter you will:

- Identify ways in which the catechetical ministry is a response to God's call to holiness.

- Use a catechetical method based on Jesus' catechetical style and methodology.

- Name the important roles of the catechist in religious education.

Second Edition

Copyright © Glencoe, Macmillan/McGraw-Hill

$\mathcal{P}$art I $\mathcal{E}$xperience

"Receive the Gospel, the Good News of Jesus Christ, the Son of God."

"God Is Calling Me to This Role"

Vocation literally means "calling." We believe that God calls us to use our talents and gifts to make life better for all. Because a vocation is a response to our natural talents and gifts, a true vocation allows us to do what makes us happy. Callings, like those to catechetical ministry, are recognized as being vocational responses and opportunities for holiness.

It was a typical Sunday in so many ways. As she gathered with the other men and women on the church steps, Miriam wondered about her place there. "Am I qualified for this?" she thought.

Miriam knew she was here because of her daughter's questions about Jesus. Mary Elizabeth was only eight, but she was certainly able to think. "Mommy, why did Jesus have to die?" "Why do we ask God to 'lead us not into temptation'? Why would God want to trick us?" Miriam was constantly challenged by Mary Elizabeth's questions, and had actually learned much about her own faith in an effort to find the proper answers for her precocious daughter. Miriam even wondered who was the real teacher here: herself or Mary Elizabeth!

Miriam felt that if her children were to love God, they would learn this primarily at home. So she showered them with love and encouragement. She spoke often of God's love and kindness. She had, however, left the children's formal religious formation in the hands of the parish catechists.

At Mass on the third Sunday in August, Father Frank spoke of the importance of Christian witness. As he ended the homily, Father Frank mentioned that parishioners were needed as teachers in the parish's religious education program. Miriam wondered if God was calling her to continue with other children the work she had already begun with Mary Elizabeth and her other children. Later that afternoon, reality set in. "Me, a teacher?" Miriam thought, "No way." However, when Mrs. Dalton, the parish Director

▲ *Being a catechist is one of the most important things that you can ever do.*

of Religious Education, phoned later in the week, Miriam listened with interest. After the conversation, Miriam realized that she had agreed to be a catechist for the third grade children. She wasn't sure whether she should be happy or panic!

Miriam had doubts about becoming a catechist. Who was she to take responsibility for the faith of other children? But as she thought of her work with Mary Elizabeth, Miriam realized that she was already a catechist in some ways. If more children could experience God's love or come to know Jesus through her, maybe she should commit herself to this task. Was this God's way of calling her to work for the kingdom?

Now, the time for doubts was over. In a few minutes she would be commissioned as a parish catechist. As Mass began, she found comfort in the Gospel reading:

> *"Whoever receives one child such as this in my name, receives me; and whoever receives me, receives not me but the One who sent me" (Mark 9:35, 37).*

"Without me, there would be no one to 'receive' these third graders this year," Miriam thought. She was excited by the challenge at hand.

All of the catechists came forward to the sanctuary when called. As the pastor's blessing rang out, Miriam looked to the congregation, and especially to her husband and children, as they extended their hands in unison. It was a good feeling to be blessed by the community for this important work.

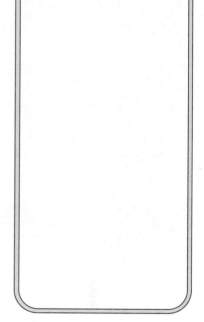

Memo

Write: Important lessons learned from catechists.

YOUR STORY

Describe your own "call" to be a catechist. How is it similar to or different from Miriam's story?

_____

_____

_____

_____

Who has influenced you the most in your decision to be a religious educator?

_____

_____

_____

_____

How does the passage (above) from Mark 9:35, 37 influence you as a catechist?

_____

_____

_____

_____

Rooted in Jesus

Most people become catechists because of their love for the students and their love for God. This love is at the heart of Christ's message; catechists need to be a living picture of that message for the students they teach. Catechists model God's love and bring the Good News to life in the lives of their students. This is the first and foremost goal of religious education and the primary reason for being a catechist.

Before you pack up your books and go home saying, "Well, I guess I can't be a catechist. I'm not perfect, so I can't ever be a perfect model of God's love," remember that if perfection was required no one could ever be a catechist. Don't be afraid to be human. Catechists model God's love best by witnessing to God through their humanity.

Jesus came to testify to God's love. Simply put, Jesus' message is Good News because it is based on God's love. The greatest of all commandments, Jesus reiterated, is "You shall love the Lord, your God, with all your heart, with all your soul, and with all your mind. . . . The second is like it: You shall love your neighbor as yourself" *(Matthew 22:37–38)*.

It is impossible to teach love. Rather, a catechist must be a person of love. Good News is shared in an atmosphere of joy. This does not mean a catechist must put on false airs and act in a way that is not compatible with his or her personality. Being "joyful" does not equate with being "giddy" or "bubbly." Rather, a joyful person communicates a peace and hopefulness for life that can only be witnessed by a person who has been touched by and accepted God's love. Be yourself; witness the joy you feel to your students.

Just about anything can be accomplished in an atmosphere of love. Parents have proved this in the rearing of their children. Even mothers and fathers with little or no parenting skills can be successful if their home is filled with love. If love has been communicated to a child from infancy, the child is likely to develop into a trusting, caring, loving person, too.

The primary mission of the catechist is to communicate God's love to each student by proclaiming the Good News of Jesus Christ. The focus of Jesus' ministry was never himself, but always the love of the Father.

Pause a Moment . . .

- What "signs of God's love" do you see around you? Why do you interpret these as signs of God's love?
- How is your life a sign of the love that God has for you?

Jesus' Teaching Method

What else can be learned from Jesus about effective catechesis? How can you incorporate the lessons learned from Jesus' methods of teaching into your own ministry? These are some of the issues that need to be considered to understand the role of catechist.

Memo

What is your response to the questions on this page? After writing your answers, share them with a friend.

To Teach as Jesus Did

In 1972, the Roman Catholic Bishops of the United States in their pastoral letter, "To Teach as Jesus Did," said:

"Religious truth must be communicated in a relevant manner which gives each student a vital experience of faith. But it must also be transmitted fully and accurately. There is no opposition between orthodoxy and relevance" (#54).

"In our world and in our nation, the mission of Christian education is of critical importance. The truth of Jesus Christ must be taught; the love of Jesus Christ must be extended to persons who seek and suffer" (#154).

Jesus' mission to humankind did not include inventing a new catechetical approach. Neither does the catechetical style of Jesus require today's catechist to learn an entirely new teaching method.

In fact, Jesus was faithful in his use of the established methods of the rabbis of his day. He abided by the traditions established by the prophets. He said, "Do not think that I have come to abolish the law or the prophets. I have come not to abolish but to fulfill" *(Matthew 5:18)*. A difference in Jesus' method with those previous is His insistence that all teaching be rooted in the interior spirit of the Jewish Law rather than the performance of external actions.

Pause a Moment . . .

- Make a list of what you consider to be the strengths of the traditional teaching methods. How can you apply these strengths to your own teaching situation?

- What do you understand by "interior spirit"? How can you apply this to your lessons? How do your students benefit from your concern?

Conversion

Jesus does not force on his listeners the truths of faith. Rather, he prepares them for a personal conversion by clearing away the anxiety and sense of unworthiness of their prior life. Jesus offers forgiveness and healing. From that starting point, those who hear him are called to personal conversion. They are constantly called to begin their lives anew.

All religious education builds upon the free faith response of the individual. Catechists help us give voice to our faith experience. Through catechesis we see life as revealing God's goodness. Catechesis helps us respond freely to God's love.

Jesus accomplished this by accepting people for who they were. Among his companions were prostitutes and tax collectors. He did not scold the woman caught in adultery, but, rather, encouraged her to change her life and to start over.

Jesus calls us to be his disciples. The perfect disciple is the person who is willing to "take up his cross and follow me." Fortunately, Jesus accepts

The New Commandment

Prior to his death and resurrection, Jesus instructed his disciples in the most important—and basic—teaching, "I give you a new commandment: love one another. As I have loved you, so you shall also love one another. This is how all will know that you are My disciples, if you have love for one another"

(John 13:34-35).

▲ *Just as this carver learned his skills at the hands of a teacher, we, too, can learn to become disciples from following Jesus' way.*

our shortcomings, knowing that each of us will be reminded of his teaching at a point in our lives when we are ready to comply. He said: "I have told you this while I am with you. The Advocate, the Holy Spirit that the Father will send in my name—he will teach you everything and remind you of all that I have told you" *(John 14:25-26)*.

Pause a Moment . . .

- How can a catechist communicate an attitude of welcoming and acceptance to his or her students?

- What changes would you need to make in your teaching style if you were to put more emphasis on the faith lives of your students? How would this affect how you planned lessons and set learning goals?

▲ *Children learn developmentally, as they are ready.*

The Way of the Cross

Jesus' method of teaching is also developmental; that is, he never tells his disciples more than they are ready to accept. This method forms the core of Mark's Gospel. The disciples clamor to know who Jesus is and what he has come to do, but the message is revealed only as the disciples can accept it. When Jesus finally does inform Peter and the others that his mission is to suffer, be rejected, and be killed, Peter is not yet ready for the truth *(Mark 8:33)*.

Even just prior to his arrest, Jesus is unwilling to let his followers in on all that awaits them. "I have much more to tell you, but you cannot bear it now. But when he comes, the Spirit of truth, he will guide you to all truth" *(John 16:12–13)*. Jesus acts in deference to their individual readiness to accept what is a radical way of life—the way of the Cross.

Jesus' method of teaching raises two important points for modern catechists: (1) It is not necessary to teach everything about the faith each year. Rather the faith is taught developmentally, presented to young students, or to students who are young in faith, as they are ready to accept it. (2) Students are to be prepared to remain open to the coming of the Holy Spirit in their lives. In this way, catechists make faith "living, conscious, and active through the light of instruction" *(NCD, #32)*. This is also the saving grace for catechists; no catechist needs to feel that he or she has to do it all in the short time allotted. Every catechists adds a little to the preparation of the students before passing them on to new hands.

Pause a Moment . . .

- How can you, as a catechist, respond to Jesus' call to "pick up your cross and follow"?

- What are some ways that the Holy Spirit is active in your own life? How would you be able to communicate this to your students?

An Invitation

Jesus' catechetical method leads each individual to make a free choice of commitment to life in God. The words and actions of Jesus all seem to have a deeper meaning; viewed as a whole they help people to believe in the mercy and goodness of God. Today we refer to this part of the catechetical process as *Evangelization*.

John's Gospel contains seven dramatic signs. These wondrous teaching lessons are done for the benefit of the learner. They provide more evidence of God's love for married couples, for the sick, for the sinful, and for the spiritually dead. In each case, it is God's love that conquers. The final sign, the raising of Lazarus *(John 11)*, foreshadows the death and resurrection of Jesus. Ironically, it is Jesus' actions in raising Lazarus that leads to his arrest.

Jesus' technique is a difficult one to master, but is an appropriate one for all catechists to follow. You can:

- Tell dramatic and powerful stories.
- Share Jesus' actions and lessons at every opportunity.
- Never force the students into a predetermined response. Help students to respond to God's love honestly and, as their catechist, accept their response.
- Prepare students to make choices appropriate to their own level of personal development.

Remember: The persuasive power of **witness** is stronger than any logical argument you can offer. In other words, your actions will speak louder than your words.

Pause a Moment...

- Why is freedom an important part of religious education?
- What are some examples of "teaching opportunities" that you have found in the lives of your students?
- What are the advantages of allowing students to freely choose or freely reject the Gospel message?

Notes

_____
_____
_____
_____
_____
_____
_____
_____
_____
_____
_____
_____
_____
_____
_____

▲ *Jesus, and his way of teaching, should be at the center of all catechesis.*

Part III Discovery

The Role of the Catechist in Religious Education

A catechist is a person of faith who has the task of creating the atmosphere for the Holy Spirit to bring about growth in faith among believers. The catechist is a person who "fosters mature faith" *(NCD, #33)* through a regular, systematic presentation. Dr. Thomas Groome, a noted religious educator, says that the catechist helps students to "make connections between their own personal story and The Story of the Christian Community, to see their own story writ large."

Catechists are engaged in the process of catechesis.

> *"Catechesis refers to efforts which help individuals and communities acquire and deepen Christian faith and identity through initiation rites, instruction, and formation of conscience. It includes both the message presented and the way it is presented"* *(NCD, #5).*

This is accomplished through the fourfold activities of Message, Community, Worship, and Service.

Fr. Berard Marthaler describes the tasks of catechesis as threefold:

- To help others grow in their personal faith and spirituality.

- To initiate others into the faith community, into its life, its worship, symbols, and practices.

- To pass on a world view, a set of shared meanings and values that are Catholic and Christian.

The role of the catechist is central to continuing the life of the Church. The message communicated by the catechist is not his or her own. It is not

---

The Catechist Has . . .

The following personal traits are essential to the role of the catechist. On a scale from 1 to 10, with 10 being the best, rate how well you fulfill these traits. The catechist has:

_____ an active faith life expressed in the worshipping community.

_____ an interest and concern about people's growth in faith.

_____ an ability to relate well with others.

_____ an integration of prayer into one's personal life.

_____ a willingness to be of service to the Church.

_____ a sense of humor and the flexibility to adapt to learning situations.

In what areas are you the strongest? In what areas do you need to improve?

invented, but experienced in faith within and through the community of believers called the Church. The parish itself serves a catechetical function. Through its commitment to living and proclaiming the Gospel, the parish is a witness to God's love. Through our experience of Church at the parish level we learn that God loves each one of us like a most-loving parent, and through the Son of the loving Father, Jesus, we are called to respond to love as mature adults.

The message of love makes real demands on the catechist. It is not enough to present the message in a convincing manner. Rather, catechists must demonstrate by their whole attitude that they are convinced of this life-giving message. This is done through a positive and appreciative approach to life and to people.

Pause a Moment . . .

- How can catechists demonstrate that they are convinced of this "life-giving message"?

- What visible signs or marks or Catholic Christian identity would you look for in your students to indicate their initiation into the faith community?

The Church Teaches

The *Catechism of the Catholic Church* teaches that catechists must be clear about the joy of Christ's way and the demands he makes. Catechists will proclaim the Holy Spirit and will, through the Spirit, inspire, guide, correct, and strengthen the lives of those whom they touch.

What Does a Catechist Do?

Catechists design and structure experiences with students that promote learning. Practicing the following five skills will help you improve the way that you design and structure learning experiences and thus help you communicate the Good News more effectively:

1. Clearly identify the specific points to be presented in each lesson in terms of the students' outcomes.

2. Understand how your students think, feel, and act in all areas of their lives.

3. Select and devise approaches that help the students to understand and to relate to the message.

4. Direct varied learning experiences and faith-growing opportunities for students.

5. Develop a method for evaluating the effectiveness of the sessions you conduct.

Becoming a catechist is not a matter of learning how to do something **to** the student. Rather, it is learning how to do something **with** the student. The emphasis today is on relationship. The catechist is seen as a witness to and a prophet of the message communicated. Therefore, the relationship between the catechist and the student is most important if the content or the techniques used are to be of value.

Pause a Moment . . .

- Summarize in your own words how each of the above five skills are related to your own particular teaching experience.

- Which of the skills listed above do you hope to develop more fully through catechist formation?

Notes

_____
_____
_____
_____
_____
_____
_____
_____
_____
_____
_____
_____
_____
_____
_____

▲ *It takes years of practice to become proficient in any craft, including catechesis.*

The Need for Formation

It is essential that catechists take time to learn more about the faith they want to share and about the art of sharing it personally and effectively. The response to the call of being a catechist "includes a willingness to give time and talent, not only to catechizing others, but to one's own continued growth in faith and understanding" *(NCD, #206).*

Goodwill alone does not ensure success in the role of catechist. A living, active faith does not necessarily include the basic teaching skills necessary to be a catechist. Busy volunteers as well as professional teachers need catechist formation.

The role of the catechist is complex. Catechists must be willing and able to learn theological and doctrinal information and make it accessible to their students. But there's more to the catechetical process then that. Catechists also model a faith-filled way of living. Catechesis aims for conversion and helping people live out their conversion.

To summarize, catechists:

- Are real, interesting, and concerned human beings.
- Have an honest awareness of themselves as people.
- Are aware of their call to be witnesses to the faith.
- Understand their students' search for values.

As catechists, the challenge is to help the students become convinced of the gift of salvation, to help them to see its consequences for everyday living, and to help them spread the Good News. When catechists are properly trained in the most effective catechetical methods, they are able to communicate the Gospel message effectively to those they teach.

Pause a Moment . . .

- How would you define "catechesis" today from your experience?
- Describe a situation in which a particular audience was challenged by the Gospel message.

You Are Important

The role of catechist that you have undertaken or are considering is a vital ministry to the Church. It is a gift that also has tremendous value for the world community at large. Through your word and action, the message of Christ continues to have a place in all human affairs.

To grow as a catechist, it is important that you:

- Be supported in your efforts.
- Continually listen to God speaking to you about the importance of your life and ministry.
- Seek out and get to know the other catechists in your parish community, arranging times to encourage one another and to affirm each other's efforts.

Your efforts as a catechist may often be taken for granted. The pressures and daily tasks of family life, work, and lesson planning may, at times, make you anxious or frustrated. At other times, you may simply lose interest or

Catechist or Teacher?

Do you see yourself as a catechist or as a teacher of religion? While often used synonymously, the words do have different meanings. Generally speaking, all catechists are teachers of religion, but not all teachers of religion are catechists.

Whether you are a teacher in a Catholic school or in a Parish School of Religion, if your goal is the faith growth of your students, then you are a catechist.

Then and Now

How have catechetical methods changed during the last 100 years? The following offers a brief glimpse at the various methods.

- **Baltimore Catechism 1885–1955**

Audience: Catholic Immigrants and defensive Catholic communities.

Intent: Unify Church through common course of study.

Approach: Dogmatic. Content presented through nearly 500 questions and answers under headings of **Creed, Commandment,** and **Sacrament and Prayer.**

Method: Repetition and memorization.

Success Criteria: Students could recite answers from memory.

- **Kerygmatic Approach 1955–1965**

Audience: Youths in established Catholic parishes.

Intent: To situate the truths of the faith in a historical context so that students could connect faith and doctrine to daily life.

Approach: Bible present as the record of God's "Good News," Liturgy was Christ's continuing presence with us.

Method: Class instruction connecting faith with world.

Success Criteria: Students understood material and remembered it longer. Students would personally live out the Gospel message.

- **Experiential Approach 1965 to the Present**

Audience: Students in changing world under pressure from competing sets of values.

Intent: Integrate faith and life experiences.

Approach: (1) Students are asked to reflect on some aspect of their own experience. (2) Catechist presents some of the content of the faith drawn from the Bible, liturgy, doctrine, or morality. (3) Catechist leads students to discover the connection between their lives and the message God is communicating to them.

Method: Shared faith stories.

Success Criteria: Full participation in Christian Life.

What can you take from each of the methods above to improve your teaching?

---

grow tired. In those moments, try to recall the catechist who had the most influence on your own faith life. Or, focus on the child who allowed you a glimpse of the face of God or the student who pursued a question with genuine interest. Let those thoughts remind you of your value; you are an important person!

Pause a Moment . . .

- How are you supported as a catechist by your parish? your family and friends? other catechists?

- What experiences encourage you to continue in your ministry as catechist? Which experience is the most discouraging?

▲ *The experiential approach to catechesis uses the children's experiences to proclaim God's word. How could this situation lead to a "teachable moment"?*

Notes

Complete the following questionnaire regarding your view of the role of catechist. If you are in a group, share your rankings with the other members of your group.

Rank the following statements in order of importance. Number 1 is the most important. Number 10 is the least important.

_____ A. A catechist is a facilitator of learning.

_____ B. A catechist relates subject matter to life.

_____ C. A catechist is a mediator and interpreter of faith.

_____ D. A catechist encourages Christian action.

_____ E. A catechist engages in serious personal study in order to participate in the Church's teaching ministry.

_____ F. A catechist is a link with the parish community.

_____ G. A catechist is aware of the social climate and peer group relationships in his or her group or class.

_____ H. A catechist recognizes the need for silence, for stillness, and non-verbal communication in the process of faith-growth.

_____ I. A catechist's goal is to transmit all of faith in an unquestioning way to the students.

_____ J. Other. _____

What you ranked highly are important values for you as you approach the ministry of catechesis. These will likely be descriptive of your personal style as a catechist.

▲ *Catechists are also learners themselves, people who never stop trying to grow in their own faith.*

$\mathcal{P}$art IV $\mathcal{R}$esponse

Miriam, the Catechist

Miriam, from the story that opened this chapter, had been a catechist for her own children long before she was called (literally and figuratively) by her parish to be a catechist for other children. When she was commissioned on Catechetical Sunday, the parish acknowledged her contribution to the faith life of the Church.

Being selected or commissioned by the Church does not make one a catechist, although these are part of the process. What makes one a catechist is a love for Jesus, the Church, and the Faith, the desire and willingness to share that love with others, and, finally, a process or method that will help the person pass along his or her love, knowledge, and wisdom to others.

We have already seen that catechists are to "teach as Jesus did." Let's look at the catechetical process that Jesus used and see how it should shape the work of the catechist even today.

▲ To become better acquainted with Jesus' story, join a Bible study group or take a Scripture class.

The "Road" to Catechesis

Catechists look to Luke 24:13–35 as the clearest example of Jesus' approach to teaching. You know the story as the "Road to Emmaus." Let's examine this story to see how Jesus taught.

On Easter Sunday, two disciples are traveling from Jerusalem to the village of Emmaus seven miles away. As they journeyed, they spoke about what had happened over the past week. As they were walking, they met a man whom they didn't recognize. The stranger asked them to tell him the story, which they did.

The stranger, who is, of course, Jesus, then proceeds to explain to them the meaning of the events that they had experienced in light of the Scriptures. It is only after they stop for a meal that the disciples come to recognize Jesus as their teacher. When they understood what had happened, they ran back to Jerusalem to tell the other disciples what they had learned.

Understanding the Process

The story illustrates the four steps of Jesus' method:

1. Human Experience
2. Message
3. Discovery
4. Response

Most of the catechetical materials used today have been developed around these same points, including this program, *Catechists in Formation*. As you learn to teach using these four steps, you will become a better catechist. You will not only be able to use your textbook more effectively as a teaching tool, but you will also be more effective in passing on your love for Jesus and the Church. Let's look at these four points in more detail.

1. Human Experience

Jesus does not start his teaching from the Scriptures or from doctrine. Rather, he starts with the faith experience of his listeners: "What are you discussing as you walk along?" *(Luke 24:17)*. Effective catechesis begins with the issues that concern six year olds, sixteen year olds, or sixty-six year olds, and allows the learners to tell their stories. The catechist teaching from a program will know prior to the class what the intended outcome of a session should be, but cannot really know what will be accomplished until he or she explores the students' experiences.

2. Message

Jesus does not even begin to explain the meaning of the passion events until after he has heard how the disciples understood those events. When the disciples finished their story, however, Jesus wasted no time in helping them understand the truth. "Then beginning with Moses and all the prophets, he interpreted to them what referred to him in all the scriptures" *(Luke 24:27)*. It is the role of the catechist to build upon the faith experience of the listener in order to help the listener interpret the meaning of Scripture and Church teaching.

3. Discovery

Good teachers do more than provide a stream of information for their students, enforce rules of discipline, or implement lesson plans. Good teachers help learners make discoveries for themselves. The same is true for good catechists; they help learners come to understand the love of God, and the meaning of our tradition for their lives.

The sense of discovery is found in the Emmaus story as well. "And so it happened that, while he was with them at table, he took bread, said the blessing, broke it, and gave it to them. With that their eyes were opened and they recognized him, but he vanished from their sight" *(Luke 24:31)*. The role of the catechist is to help the learner recognize Jesus through their life experiences and the teaching of the Church.

Catechist Checklist

The following are a few actions and characteristics often associated with a catechist. The effective catechist will:

1. Read and prepare the lesson prior to the next meeting with the students.

2. Strive to learn each student's name as quickly as possible in order to greet each by name when they arrive for class.

3. Maintain eye contact with the entire group as he or she moves from section to section of the lesson.

4. Show patience as students struggle to put ideas into words.

5. Think about each and every student and attempt to make concrete connections to his or her life.

6. Prepare each part of the lesson and check it twice before class begins. Preview all audio-visuals. Make sure that all equipment works prior to class.

7. Prior to entering the class setting, say a quiet prayer to the Holy Spirit.

What else is needed to make a successful catechist? Write your suggestions on the lines below.

4. Response

Jesus called forth a response from the listener. "Were not our hearts burning [within us] while he spoke to us on the way and opened the scriptures for us?" *(Luke 24:35)*.

Every lesson should lead to a response of some kind. While the catechist may encourage students to action, it is here that the catechist's faith in God is most evident. No catechist, not even Jesus himself, can control how another person will act. All the catechist can do is prepare lessons that lead and encourage the student to take action.

Take a moment to consider the following reflection exercise. Then, think about how this learning process works in your own life.

- Reflect on a time when God became more real to you. How did you learn in this situation?

- Was there a passage from scripture or an element from our Tradition that helped you to make sense of this experience?

- How did you see yourself in the scripture? What connection did you make with our Tradition? What did you discover?

- How did you act on this discovery?

CATECHIST JOB DESCRIPTION

Now that you have read and reflected on the ministry of the catechist in today's Church, develop a catechist's job description:

Wanted: Catechist

Role (What tasks does a catechist perform?):

_____

_____

Requirements (What qualities should a catechist have in order to be successful?):

_____

_____

Compensation (What rewards can a catechist expect? Why would someone want to be a catechist?):

_____

_____

_____

Write a brief statement explaining why you feel that you are a catechist:

_____

_____

_____

_____

_____

_____

Catechetical Guidance

The Church has provided much guidance to catechists over the past 30 years. The following is a list of some of the most important of those documents:

- *The Documents of the Second Vatican Council,* 1962–65.
- *The General Catechetical Directory,* Sacred Congregation of the Clergy, 1971.
- *To Teach as Jesus Did,* United States Catholic Conference, 1972.
- *Evangelii Nuntiandi,* Pope Paul VI, 1975.
- *Sharing the Light of Faith,* (The National Catechetical Directory). United States Catholic Conference, 1979.
- *Catechesi Tradendae,* Pope John Paul II, 1979.
- *Guidelines for Doctrinally Sound Catechetical Materials,* United States Catholic Conference, 1990.

Prayer Response

Music can be a powerful instrument of conversion. Gregorian chant, "Handel's Messiah," or even worship music by the St. Louis Jesuits can carry our hearts to God. Whether you teach primary, junior high, or marriage preparation courses, your students will almost always be immersed in popular music. It is the wise catechist who tunes in to this secular music and uses it to convey messages of faith.

Listen to a song your students like. Compose a prayer response to those words. Use the song and prayer with your students. Have them compose similar prayers for their favorite songs.

BIBLIOGRAPHY

DeGidio, Sandra, O.S.M. "Helping Our Children Grow in Faith," *Catholic Update,* St. Anthony Messenger Press, September, 1982.

Diocese of Salt Lake City. *Basic Course for Catechist Formation.* "Catechists Yesterday and Today." Video.

Groome, Thomas. *Christian Religious Education.* San Francisco: Harper & Row, 1980.

Kelly, Francis D., *The Mystery We Proclaim, Catechesis at the Third Millennium.* Huntington, IN: Our Sunday Visitor, 1993.

Manternach, Janaan and Pfeifer, Carl J. *Creative Catechist.* West Mystic, CT: Twenty-Third Publications, 1991. Especially the Introduction and Chapters 1, 2, 3, and 4.
    How To Be a Better Catechist. Kansas City: Sheed & Ward, 1989.

Moran, Gabriel. *Education toward Adulthood: Religion and Lifelong Learning.* Mahwah, NJ: Paulist Press, 1979.

Murphy, Msgr. John Francis. "A Catechist Is," *The Religion Teacher's Handbook.* Milwaukee: Hi Time Publishers, Inc. 1978.

O'Malley, William J. SJ, *Becoming a Catechist: Ways to Outfox Teenage Skepticism.* Mahwah, NJ: Paulist Press, 1993.

National Conference of Catholic Bishops. "Chapter II, The Catechetical Ministry of the Church; Chapter IX, Catechetical Personnel." *Sharing the Light of Faith: National Catechetical Directory for Catholics of the United States.* Washington, DC: USCC Publications, 1979.
    To Teach As Jesus Did. Washington, DC: USCC Publications, 1973.

Religion Teacher's Training Program. Session #1, "The Ministry of the Catechist." West Mystic, CT: Twenty-Third Publications. 25 minute video.

Sacred Congregation for the Clergy. *General Catechetical Directory.* Washington, DC: USCC Publications, 1971.

Schippe, Cullen. *Planting, Watering, Growing—Volunteer Catechist's Companion.* Los Angeles: Sandalprints, 1990.

Nihil Obstat
The Reverend Robert D. Lunsford, M. A.

Imprimatur
The Most Reverend Kenneth J. Povish, D. D.
Bishop of Lansing
June 24, 1993

The *Nihil Obstat* and *Imprimatur* are official declarations that a book or pamphlet is free of doctrinal or moral error. No implication is contained therein that those who have granted the Nihil Obstat and Imprimatur agree with the contents, opinions, or statements expressed.

Scripture passages are taken from *The New American Bible with Revised New Testament,* copyright © 1988 by the Confraternity of Christian Doctrine, Washington, D.C. All rights reserved.

Copyright © 1994 by the Glencoe Division of Macmillan/McGraw-Hill School Publishing Company. All rights reserved. Except as permitted under the United States Copyright Act, no part of this publication may be reproduced or distributed in any form or by any means, or stored in a database or retrieval system, without the prior written permission of the publisher.

This chapter may be ordered separately using the following ISBN number.

Send all inquiries to:
BENZIGER PUBLISHING COMPANY
15319 Chatsworth Street
P.O. Box 9609
Mission Hills, California 91346-9609

Second Edition

ISBN 0-02-651191-6

Printed in the United States of America.

1 2 3 4 5 6 7 8 9 BAW 97 96 95 94 93

Benziger

Understanding How Faith Develops

As the National Catechetical Directory recognizes, the purpose of catechesis is to make a person's "faith become living, conscious, and active, through the light of instruction" (NCD, #32) using whatever methods are necessary to achieve this goal. Because every person—child, adolescent, or adult—comes to catechesis already with faith, even if only a minimal amount, catechists take the initial faith of their students, enrich it, and help it grow.

BOOK ONE

In this chapter you will:

- Chart the milestones of your own faith life and point out their importance to your development.

- Describe the dimensions of faith and distinguish between faith, religion, and belief.

- Identify ways that mature faith can be put into action and measure your own level of faith development.

- Apply strategies for using the proper age level techniques with your students to help them grow in faith.

Second Edition

Copyright © Glencoe, Macmillan/McGraw-Hill

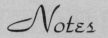

Part I Experience

Early One Sunday Morning

As George Martin prepared for his Sunday morning shower and shave, he knew that larger than usual problems lay ahead. Lately, it had become a real battle for him to assemble 17-year-old Matt, 13-year-old Kari, and 8-year-old Michael together for Sunday Mass and family activities on the alternate weekends they stayed with him.

Matt, in his first year of community college, worked at a gas station on most Sunday mornings. He was off to work this morning, "Don't worry, Dad, I'll hit the Newmann Center Mass on my way home." With Michael, George would promise that after Mass they could throw the ball around or play a game. Kari, however, was a different matter.

From the time she was little, Kari was the typical "Daddy's girl." She loved doing things and going places with her father. Even an errand to the hardware store was a special time for Kari to be with her dad. Mass with dad was one of Kari's favorites, and she always dressed for the occasion. With a glance into Kari's room, George knew that she did not plan to go to Mass today. She wore her running shoes with jeans and a T-shirt. As she brushed her hair, her expression was stern as if already anticipating the confrontation she knew was soon to come.

"I'm not going to church today," Kari said.

"Is there a problem?" George asked. "Will you kindly explain to me the reason for that comment?"

Kari responded, "The people are not friendly there. They give you a phony smile at the beginning of Mass, and then race to their cars and ignore you after it's over. And I'm not sure if I even believe in God anymore."

Kari started to cry. George knew the divorce was bothering her again. Two years had elapsed, yet Kari was still sensitive to the relationship between him and her mother. Kari had always been so full of hope, but now George didn't know what to expect.

"Dad, I have to go," Kari said, checking carefully to make sure that she had wiped away all her tears. Sure enough, a car horn blasted from out in front. She **really** was not going to go to Mass. George asked were she was going.

"You know about this, Daddy, you're one of my sponsors. Don't you remember?" Kari said, looking right at him. Of course, George remembered, the AIDS walk-a-thon was today. Kari and her friends from school had raised over $2000 for AIDS research and hospice care.

"Kari," George said. "You can go on the walk, but why all the big fuss about Mass? You don't believe the things you said, do you?"

"Daddy, I wasn't kidding. I really am confused. When we're with you, we go to the morning Mass. When we're with Mom, we go to the night Mass so that you two won't run into each other. And then you both try to tell us about this loving, forgiving God. "I once hoped that everything would be better, but now I'm not sure if anything in this world will ever be right again," she added.

The car horn blared again. "Dad, I have to go."

Notes

_____
_____
_____
_____
_____
_____
_____
_____
_____
_____
_____
_____

Quickly jot down your responses to the following questions, answering as you feel at this moment.

1. What do I believe about God, Jesus, the Church, and the meaning of human life?

_____

_____

_____

_____

2. Why do I believe what I believe?

_____

_____

_____

_____

3. How do I feel about questioning and doubting my beliefs?

_____

_____

_____

_____

4. How have I struggled (as Kari did) to understand what I believe ?

_____

_____

_____

_____

Memo

How do I distinguish between faith and belief?

▲ *Adolescents, like Kari, look for ways to put their faith into action. They care deeply for others in need.*

Defining Faith

What do you think of when you hear the word, "faith"? Would you describe faith as the truths you believe in, or as the doctrines taught by the Church? Perhaps you would describe faith as believing in something without being able to prove it. Or, perhaps you'd say it is the way you live, or the things you *must* believe, or the things that God has revealed.

Faith can mean different things for different people. There are people who were reared in Catholic homes, taught their religious traditions, and given good example, who later deny the existence of God and reject the Church's beliefs. There are other people, however, who came from families were God was mocked—if thought of at all—who now are devoted members of the Church. Why do some have this mysterious experience of faith while others do not?

1. **Faith is first, and foremost, a gift from God.** It cannot be given from one person to another. It cannot be earned, merited, or manufactured.

2. **Faith is personal.** It reflects an individual's personal relationship with a living, active God.

3. **Faith is active and requires risk-taking.** Faith deals with realities for which the evidence in not clear. Faith moves people to go beyond their comfortable level of living. Faith challenges people to act for God and others.

4. **Faith is a way of seeing reality.** Faith provides a lens through which people view life. With faith, things have a way of fitting together into a meaningful picture. Ordinary events become more significant.

5. **Faith has an ecclesial dimension as well.** Faith is lived out in community. We grow in faith through the example of others; strengthened through their witness. The Church, too, through its teaching authority (*magisterium*) and pastoral leaders, offers us guidance for growing in faith.

6. **Faith is developmental.** Faith grows and matures in the same way that people grow and mature, although faith does not necessarily grow and mature at the same pace as physical or moral maturity.

In short, *faith is the essential way humans confront reality as free and responsible beings.* According to psychologist Dr. James Fowler, an expert in the study of how faith develops, faith is the process of finding meaning and truth at the most fundamental level in which all human beings engage. Faith is a basic relationship to something or someone that transcends the individual. It is the reference point to a person's life. For Catholics and other Christians, faith commonly expresses one's relationship with God through Jesus Christ.

▲ *Special moments, like a wedding or the birth of a child, can be experiences of faith.*

Pause a Moment . . .

- How do the above definitions of faith resonate with your experience?
- Which element of faith best fits your own life? Explain.

Faith, Religion, and Belief

You were asked earlier to identify how you distinguish between religion and belief. Go back and review what you wrote.

Dr. Fowler, mentioned earlier, distinguishes religion from faith by saying that religion is the belief in and living out of the "cumulative tradition" and vast scope of the community's faith. This definition would include the many expressions of the faith of people in the past and of the present. Scripture and theology, symbol and myth, ethical teachings and prayer, architecture and music, art and patterns of teaching and preaching are all parts of religion. Individually, people with religious faith use the elements of religion as aids to form and give expression to their personal relationship with God. Pretty complex, isn't it?

As a catechist all you need to remember is that while "belief" is often used interchangeably with "faith," they are not the same thing.

- Faith is the recognition that certain ideas are true.

- Belief is the assent to the ideas accepted in faith.

- Religion is the living out of one's beliefs.

Faith and religious belief do work together for the betterment of each. Faith helps to vitalize and renew belief, while belief gives concrete expression to faith.

According to Fowler, faith is deeper than belief. Expressions of belief—like the Christian creeds prayed privately or in public liturgy—may accurately communicate our faith, but faith also involves deeper, unconscious motivations as well as those expressed consciously through our beliefs and actions.

Fowler's thesis is that faith is part of the generic makeup of humanity. Human beings have a need for faith from the beginning; that is, a need to form relationships of trust and loyalty to ideals or others. According to Fowler, this need evolves whether or not we are nurtured in faith in religious or Christian ways. In the heterogeneous world in which we live, faith and its expressions can take many forms.

The Second Vatican Council's *Document on Revelation* offers the following:

> *"By faith man freely commits his entire self to God, making the full submission of his intellect and will to God who reveals.'"*

The Council did not want to describe faith as simply an intellectual exercise. Rather, it recognized that faith was an action of the entire person in relationship with God. It recognized that, ultimately, faith is a commitment; a free choice we make to give ourselves to God and live in a whole new way. We are left free to accept or reject God's generous gift.

Pause a Moment . . .

- What does it mean to say that faith does not have to be limited to religious faith?

- Share an example that explains the difference between belief and faith.

- How does the distinction between faith and religion help you to better understand the discussion between Kari and her father in the opening story?

Notes

The Church Teaches

According to the *Catechism of the Catholic Church, #166*, faith is a personal, free response we make to God's invitation to us. The Catechism recognizes, however, that faith is never an isolated act. While personal, it is also always for the benefit of others just as we benefit from them.

Responding to God with Faith

In the Bible, there are stories about people of faith who were asked by God to respond in different ways:

- Moses and his people were asked to believe that God would take care of them in the desert and lead them to the land of promise.

- King David repented his adultery with Bathsheba, and the murder of her husband, when challenged by God's word through the prophet, Nathan.

- Jonah was sent to the Ninevites to urge them to repent.

- Jeremiah was called to be a prophet, though he did not feel qualified or even ready for such a responsibility.

Isaiah reminds us that the faithful person is able to trust in God's care. "Thus said the Lord God, the Holy One of Israel: By waiting and by calm you shall be saved; in quiet and in trust your strength lies" *(Isaiah 30:15).*

Isaiah describes God as eager and willing to show great love for all. "He will be gracious to you when you cry out, as soon as He hears He will answer you" *(Isaiah 30:19).*

Sometimes God's people are able to persevere in their difficulties only because they know God is with them and will deliver them. Martha and Mary faced the tragedy of their brother Lazarus's death knowing that Jesus would somehow make all things right. And Mary, the mother of Jesus, accepted the painful experience of her Son's suffering and death only because she believed in God and God's plan for the world. Obviously, for the Jews and the early Christians, faith was far more than mere belief in a body of truths.

Your challenge is not to create a new faith or a different faith in your students, but, rather, to expand on the faith that each one brings to you by introducing them to the faith of the Christian community. To do this, you must be aware of where they are in their faith journey, and adjust your presentation to their level.

Pause a Moment . . .

- How is your faith journey reflected in the stories from the Bible?

- What does it mean to say that the catechist is to introduce the students to the faith of the Christian community, not give them a new faith?

▲ *Many people are dedicated to performing acts of charity because of their faith in God.*

Your Journal

Reflect on each of the following statements and then write your answers. Share them with a fellow catechist.

1. To grow means to change. Often, there is much pain and uncertainty involved with growing in faith. What feelings do you associate with the idea of change?

_____

_____

_____

_____

2. A principal sin against faith is the refusal to question it. Living a life of faith is not necessarily consoling. It involves facing many questions and uncertainties in a changing world and a changing Church. What are your reactions to these challenges?

_____

_____

_____

_____

3. How will your students be influenced by your faith?

_____

_____

_____

▲ *How do you model your faith for your own children and for the children you teach?*

The New Commandment

"I assure you, if you had faith the size of a mustard seed, you would be able to say to this mountain, "Move from here to there," and it would move. Nothing would be impossible for you"

(Matthew 17:20–21).

What Is Mature Catholic Christian Faith?

Very often, a person, during a crisis or a moment of great significance, experiences a sudden burst of insight into the meaning of faith. The death of a loved one, sickness, crisis, the birth of a child, and family celebrations are all occasions that may offer a person an opportunity to better understand the faith. Many people have commented on their responsiveness to God at these moments. From these moments, people come to a deeper understanding and maturity of their faith.

Mature faith is a commitment. It is a free choice by which we give ourselves to God and begin living out a whole new way of life. God does not force the gift of faith upon us. It is only offered. We are left free to decide whether to accept or reject it.

For a Catholic Christian, mature faith is grounded in the saving actions of the Paschal Mystery—especially in Christ's resurrection from the dead. Saint Paul wrote: "And if Christ has not been raised, then empty [too] is our preaching; empty, too, your faith" *(1 Corinthians 15:14)*.

Mature faith is not an intellectual reality, but rather the action of a person in relationship with God. A person of mature faith lives the Gospel. Or, as the *National Catechetical Directory* says, this is a faith that is "living, conscious, and active." This living faith in the resurrection and new life is at the core of the Church's teaching. Paul pointed this out in the First Letter to the Thessalonians, "we too give thanks to God unceasingly, that, in receiving the word of God from hearing us, you received not a human word but, as it truly is, the word of God, which is now at work in you who believe" *(1 Thessalonians 2:13)*.

Pause a Moment...

- What are concrete signs of a "living, conscious, and active faith"?
- How would you measure someone's growth in faith based upon the living, conscious, and active criteria?

What Does Mature Faith Look Like?

More than a body of truths, mature faith is a response to the needs placed before us in daily life. Mature faith reflects the many different ways that faith is lived. The following vignettes taken from recent news stories offer several examples of people and groups who live out their faith. How would your story fit here? In what ways has your call to be a catechist helped you to confront your own responsibility as a participant in God's creation?

- Mother Teresa did not stay for the filet mignon dinner held in her honor by the Knights of Columbus. She asking that the money spent on this lavish dinner be given to the poor instead. The Knights complied with her request *(National Catholic Reporter)*.

- "Catholic Social Services of Indiana has developed an alternative that keeps aging parents in a loving, caring, home environment, while also providing social opportunities for them and temporary relief for the caregivers. . . .The drop-off program offers daily structured activities and limited medical care to older adults in a community atmosphere, while primary caregivers work or engage in other activities" *(Our Sunday Visitor)*.

- "With school soon to start, Saint Anne parishioners in Warren, Michigan will resume making sleeping bags for the homeless, a project they began last winter, producing 480 bags with nylon shells and flannel linings that encase warm batting" *(National Catholic Reporter)*.

Notes

How Mature Is Your Faith?

To better understand the nature of mature faith, researchers from the *Search Institute* conducted a survey among the mainline Protestant traditions. From their research, they arrived at eight dimensions that make up a mature faith. As you examine and reflect on each of the dimensions, determine how you currently meet these criteria in your own life. Write the appropriate number on the line that follows, using the following scale:

1	2	3	4	5	6	7	8	9	10
Rarely				Often					Always

A person with mature faith:

1. Trusts in God's saving grace and believes firmly in the humanity and divinity of Jesus. _____

2. Experiences a sense of personal well-being, security, and peace. _____

3. Integrates faith and life, and sees work, family, social relationships, and political choices as part of religious life. _____

4. Seeks spiritual growth through study, reflection, prayer, and discussion with others. _____

5. Seeks to be part of a community of believers in which people witness to their faith and support and nourish one another. _____

6. Holds life-affirming values, including a commitment to racial and gender equality, an affirmation of cultural and religious diversity, and a personal sense of responsibility for the welfare of others. _____

7. Advocates social and global changes to bring about greater social justice. _____

8. Serves humanity consistently and passionately through acts of love and justice. _____

(From Benson, Peter and Carolyn H. Eklin. *Effective Christian Education: A National Study of Protestant Congregations—A Summary Report on Faith, Loyalty, and Congregational Life.* Minneapolis, MN: Search Institute, 1990. Reprinted by permission.)

Pause a Moment . . .

- Which dimension of a mature faith do you consider to be most important? The least important? Why?

- Who has been an example of a resurrection person to you?

- In one sentence, give your definition of "mature faith."

▲ *What does it mean to be a person of mature faith?*

The Place of Doubt in a Life of Faith

Faith does not necessarily include a great number of comfortable short-cuts through life. As John Kirvan has stated,

> *"Faith isn't a blank check on happiness. No one ever said that if you believe the pain of being human is just going to disappear. Faith isn't a backdoor out of the human condition. Faith doesn't change the facts of life, it just lets you see them in a different light. It lets you see into them and through them. Pains don't hurt less because you know there is a God; it's just that in their midst you know that they aren't the whole story."* (The Restless Believers, p. 105.)

Moments of light, moments of shadow, times of certainty, times of doubt—all are a natural part of the life of faith. There is a wisdom in the rhythm of the positive and the negative; we need both to grow in faith and to gain a mature faith.

Pause a Moment...

- Write down how your faith is sometimes challenged.

- Describe, in writing, a personal "moment of shadow" when you had difficulty understanding a particular Church teaching or the entire notion of belief altogether. How did you grow from this experience?

▲ *Faith in God is not just for the good times.*

Places in the Journey

One of the fortunate elements of teaching is that most learning is developmental: one lesson builds for the next; one course readies a student for another. Since the Second Vatican Council, a greater emphasis has been placed on the ongoing religious and spiritual development of people, from birth to death. There has been a recognition of the importance of each stage along life's journey with the view that people are constantly readying themselves for the coming of God's reign. This understanding has dramatically affected catechesis:

> "Because the life of faith is related to human development, it passes through stages or levels; furthermore, different people possess aspects of faith to different degrees. This is true, for example, of the comprehensiveness and intensity with which they accept God's word, of their ability to explain it, and of their ability to apply it to life. Catechesis is meant to help at each stage of human development and lead ultimately to full identification with Jesus" (National Catechetical Directory, #176).

Crucial movements in the journey of faith occur at many stages. These movements or turning points are part of the process of growing faith just as movements of physical growth are marked by a baby's first steps, a kindergartner's first day of school, or the beginning of puberty for a pre-teen. Life itself creates the need to learn and we seek out formal and informal opportunities to satisfy this need.

As with other types of development, turning points in faith development offer the opportunity for and the motivation to grow and learn. In a family, there are many ways to share these opportunities and support one another in faith.

▲ *Adults can help teenagers through difficult times by caring for them and being with them.*

- Adults can help young children to gain a solid foundation in faith by the example they set for living the faith in all its aspects.

- Adults can help teenagers through their time of search, rebellion, or doubt by giving them support and understanding.

- Adults can also help one another in their turning points; they can learn from the simple faith of children and the adolescent's characteristic willingness to search and question. For the continuing development of faith, such support is crucial.

The journey of faith never ends; rather it continues to expand in new and unique directions.

Pause a Moment . . .

- List concrete ways that you can help the children you teach grow in faith.

- Why is it important to understand that faith is developmental?

Developing Faith in Youth

Where adults believe because they have discovered personal reasons for belief, children accept the gift of faith by observing and imitating the adult models in their lives. Parents, relatives, and teachers tell children what to believe, but it is their example that makes the strongest impact, because children learn about faith primarily through observation. Between childhood and adulthood, people begin to discover that the reasons to believe, which they embraced as children, may no longer seem compelling. The adolescent may not yet have found personal reasons for believing, and so may rebel against, question, or doubt what they have been taught. This is all part of the process leading to an adult faith.

Turning points like this are not limited only to adolescents. Adults at mid-life can also experience doubts of faith. One might begin to question decisions made years earlier.

Though each person is gifted with faith, George Martin's dilemma—sharing his Catholic Christian faith with his children—was greater because of the wide range of age difference between Michael, Kari, and Matt.

To Michael, an eight-year-old, the immediate family remains the main setting in his life where he experiences his relationship with God. The interplay between a father and son, and the sharing of an afternoon activity is an extremely important way to manifest the reality of God and God's love.

Seventeen-year-old Matt, on the other hand, is reaching the stage of young adulthood when men and women are most likely to sever their ties—temporarily in many cases—with organized religion. Young adults are often influenced by many subgroups of peers. Matt is more likely to attend the Newmann Center Mass at college to see a certain young lady, than he is of attending Mass to please his father.

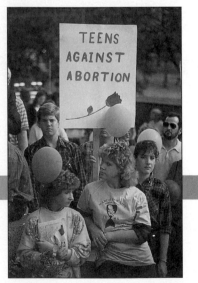

▲ *If given the opportunity and encouragement, adolescents will get involved to make a difference in the world.*

Talking about God with Children

In Rabbi Marc Gellman and Monsignor Thomas Hartman's book, *Where Does God Live?,* they outline these five principles for talking about God with children. How can you incorporate these principles into your personal catechetical setting?

1. Let your child watch you do religious things.

2. Tell your children what you believe while making it clear that they must decide what they believe.

3. Don't be afraid to say, "I don't know" when talking to your child about God.

4. Try to relate God to how we live and not just what we believe.

5. Don't give answers about God that are too simple.

Adolescence is one of the most difficult and exciting times of faith development. It is, also, often a time when religious belief and personal faith are not synchronized.

Fourteen-year-old Kari's willingness to reach out in service to those in need through her participation in the AIDS walk-a-thon is typical of the budding idealism that marks adolescence. The behavior of adults is examined more closely. The flaws of parents, teachers, and priests become magnified. In turn, any suggestion of authority from adult figures is heard with less than responsive ears.

As the primary religious educators of their children, all parents—like George Martin—face many uphill battles in preserving the religious faith traditions that have been passed on through generations in their own families. Fortunately, the task is not one that must be accomplished alone. The example and efforts of the community of faith is an ever-responsive gift to parents in need. The catechist's role in this challenge of religious education is also a crucial one.

Pause a Moment . . .

- What do you consider to be the foremost challenges facing parents today in their role as religious educators?

- What are some creative ways a parish community can support a parent's attempts to hand on the faith?

- What procedures would you recommend that your parish establish to complement and support the parents' efforts to build faith in the home?

Meeting People Where They Are

As a catechist, you are called to know and understand something of the particular stage of religious development of your students and use the appropriate teaching method best suited to their needs.

Here are some basic characteristics and suggestions for several developmental levels. Use this list as a basic framework for putting together an age-appropriate course of study in your particular specialty of catechesis.

Kindergarten to Third Grade

The *kindergarten through grade 3* student's intellectual capacity is gradually expanding. The child's view of the world is based on very direct and personal experiences. In this stage, the child develops the ability to form concrete ideas or concepts based on a variety of experiences and contacts from peers, other adults, and the media. Still, even up to eight years old, a child retains his or her sense of wonder. These children remain very open, loving, and eager to please. These combinations of developmental traits can be helpful tools to assist the child's growth in faith.

The most successful activities for K-3 students are ones that **introduce** them to various aspects of faith. Words are okay, but give them opportunities to see, touch, and experience the particular aspect of faith you are teaching. God can be experienced at all times through all the wonders of the senses and of creation. Some effective techniques include role-playing Bible stories, miming the message of a song with hand and body motions, and prayer experiences that utilize the senses and nature.

Use repetition. Sing songs, play records, and read or tell stories several times. You may get tired of these, but the students do not. It takes several hearing (singings) for them to really catch on to the activity. Have each child in your group leave his or her hand prints (in washable paint!) on a banner entitled "We Belong to God." Use this banner for worship services.

Implications of Faith

To believe in God, the only God, and to love God with one's whole being has immense consequences for every part of our life:

- It means knowing the greatness and majesty of God.
- It means living out our thanksgiving.
- It means knowing the unity and the true dignity of all.
- It means the proper use of created things.
- It means trusting God in all circumstances, even in times of adversity.

How does this implication of faith and its consequences shape your life? How have the implications of faith been tested in your life?

Fourth to Sixth Grade

Students in *grade 4 through grade 6* are approaching the time in their physical lives—preadolescence—when physical changes often make it difficult for them to come to terms with their emerging sexuality. At this stage, the peer group exerts a much greater influence. Personal freedom and the responsibilities and consequences of decision-making, along with a keen sense of justice, are other important issues to consider when working with students of this age.

Because of an increase in a preadolescent's intellectual ability, students can delve more deeply into information about the Church, sacraments, and Scripture. Presentations are a more effective tool for students of this age than they would have been at an earlier age. However, a "hands on" approach is still the best rule. Individualized and group projects, field trips, art work, and media presentations are all successful teaching tools. Also, considering students of this age are in the midst of a hero-worship stage, relating the examples and values of the saints to the overall course of study can also be of great value.

Foster the students' growing inquisitiveness and find ways to help them feel more a part of their parish. Explore creative and open-ended ways to guide them through the frequent clashes between peer values and faith values.

Seventh to Ninth Grades

Students in *grade 7 to grade 9* bring a different twist to hero worship. While they do still tend to admire famous people such as rock stars or athletes, heroes to seventh, eighth, or ninth graders are more likely to be boys or girls only a few years older than they are. Catechists of this level students may consider having older students serve as leaders where they can offer short, simple, and practical witness talks about their own faith journey.

Early adolescents remain very peer oriented and are very sensitive to what others think of them. In spite of their self-doubts and the external pressures associated with this age, these students usually develop a new spiritual outlook on life in general, on themselves, and on those around them. This growing faith awareness leads these students to a greater ability to love and to a more mature faith. Catechists do well when they stress the excitement of this age, rather than its obvious pratfalls. An increased freedom to explore new areas of life for the first time is an exciting opportunity that indicates a person's growth.

The difficulty for a catechist working with these students is that students are likely to ignore a great part of what any adult says to them, not just the catechist. At this age, the children simply have other issues on their minds, other "fish to fry." They prefer to explore answers to serious and less serious problems on their own.

This individuality needs to be respected. Remember that these students are more impressed by example than they are by words. The more they can be involved in hands-on activities, the greater will be their interest in faith issues.

Tenth to Twelfth Grade

In *grades 10 to 12*, students need reassurance that their questioning and searching is acceptable. They need opportunities to explore the implications of a subject in peer group discussions. Because students at this age are attempting to formulate their own direction and purpose, a catechist must give careful attention to the rational basis of faith. Teens are usually interested in what adults have to say; inviting a guest speaker will spark attention and interest. Students will not respond positively, however, if the speaker talks down to them.

There is a common misconception that students of this age are not interested in religious or spiritual topics. Because of this error, lessons often focus exclusively on topics of self-esteem, dating, and sexuality. In fact, studies show that high school students are most interested in learning and sharing about the crucial life and death issues that make up the deepest parts of a human being's faith experiences. Instead of being uninterested, it is actually a question of their faith not being expressed in the way or manner expected by the religion that they have received. Appropriate presentations of religious topics are usually very well received.

Students in grades 10 to 12 are very concerned for others and are willing to work on worthwhile service projects. They also are very responsive to personal witness stories and look for opportunities to build relationships. Providing service opportunities followed by a systematic debriefing can be a powerful occasion for them. Invite guests to give public witness to God's role in their lives. Have students work together in small groups to tackle projects. Participating as a group in the Eucharist and other worship services also can have a positive impact on the students' growing faith. You can also use journal writing, opportunities for reflective, personal prayer, and group retreats as effective tools to reach students of this age.

YOUR STORY

How can you apply what you've learned to your teaching? Write your responses to each of the following questions or statements.

1. How should you respond when the students ask a question about God?

_____

_____

2. What situations in your students' lives cause them to encounter and struggle with mystery? How can you assist them in their struggle?

_____

_____

3. As a catechist, how do you create an environment where faith can grow?

_____

_____

4. List some general characteristics about the students you teach. Describe two or three specific approaches for helping them to grow in faith.

_____

_____

_____

_____

▲ *What are some ways that you can make "students helping other students" part of your lesson plan?*

▲ *What can you do to help your students when they struggle to understand God's mystery?*

Memo

What is your "prayer for the faith journey"?

Prayer Response

Compose your own "prayer for the faith journey." Thank God for leading you this far by faith and ask God to continue to lead you forward. If you are with a group, take turns sharing your prayers for the journey.

BIBLIOGRAPHY

Benson, Peter and Carolyn H. Eklin. *Effective Christian Education: A National Study of Protestant Congregations.* Minneapolis, MN: Search Institute, 1990.

Cronin, Gaynell. *Effective Teaching Methods II,* "Discovering Faith." Mahwah, NJ: Paulist Press, 50-minute video.

DeGidio, Sandra, O.S.M. "Helping Our Children Grow in Faith." *Catholic Update.* Cincinnati: St. Anthony Messenger Press, September, 1982.

Fowler, James W. "Life-Faith Patterns; Structures of Trust and Loyalty," *Life Maps: Conversations on the Journey of Faith.* Edited by Jerome Berryman. Waco, TX: Word Books 1978.

Kirvan, John J. *The Restless Believers.* Mahwah, NJ: Paulist Press, 1966.

National Conference of Catholic Bishops. Chapter III and Chapter VIII, *Sharing the Light of Faith.* Washington, DC: USCC Publications, 1979.

Powell, Fr. John, SJ. *Faith: The Search for God.* Allen, TX: Tabor. Video.

Sweeney, Richard J. "How God Invites Us to Grow: Six Stages of Faith Development" *Catholic Update.* Cincinnati: St. Anthony Messenger Press, October 1987.

Westerhoff, John. *Will Our Children Have Faith?* Allen, TX: Tabor. Video.

Nihil Obstat
The Reverend Robert D. Lunsford, M.A.

Imprimatur
The Most Reverend Kenneth J. Povish, D.D.
Bishop of Lansing
June 24, 1993

The *Nihil Obstat* and *Imprimatur* are official declarations that a book or pamphlet is free of doctrinal or moral error. No implication is contained therein that those who have granted the *Nihil Obstat* and *Imprimatur* agree with the contents, opinions, or statements expressed.

Scripture passages are taken from *The New American Bible with Revised New Testament,* copyright © 1988 by the Confraternity of Christian Doctrine, Washington, D.C. All rights reserved.

Copyright © 1994 by the Glencoe Division of Macmillan/McGraw-Hill School Publishing Company. All rights reserved. Except as permitted under the United States Copyright Act, no part of this publication may be reproduced or distributed in any form or by any means, or stored in a database or retrieval system, without the prior written permission of the publisher.

This chapter may be ordered separately using the following ISBN number.

Send all inquiries to:
BENZIGER PUBLISHING COMPANY
15319 Chatsworth Street
P.O. Box 9609
Mission Hills, California 91346-9609

Second Edition

ISBN 0-02-651193-2

Printed in the United States of America.

1 2 3 4 5 6 7 8 9   BAW   97 96 95 94 93

Knowing Your Students

I've long since retired, my son's moved away. I called him up just the other day.

I said, "I'd like to see you if you don't mind." He said, "I'd love to Dad

    if I can find the time.

You see my new job's a hassle and the kids have the flu, but it's sure nice

    talkin' to you, Dad. It's been sure nice talkin' to you."

And as he hung up the phone it occurred to me—

    he'd grown up just like me. My boy was just like me.

"Cats in the Cradle" by Harry Chapin and Sandy Chapin,
©1974 Story Songs, Ltd.

In this chapter you will:

- Identify the challenges students face as they grow in faith.
- Analyze the environments that influence the lives of your students.
- Relate the various remote and proximate factors which affect faith development to your teaching ministry.

Second Edition

Copyright © Glencoe, Macmillan/McGraw-Hill

$\mathcal{P}$art I $\mathcal{E}$xperience

I Didn't Understand

The first time I met Frank was in front of the school, before the morning prayer assembly. It was halfway through the term. Frank was a new student in my seventh grade class.

"Mr. Doten, this is Francisco," Frank's father began. "Son, shake your teacher's hand." Frank kept his head down, but extended his hand.

Frank's mother was also there, but since she did not speak English, she simply nodded her greeting. As his parents left, I said, "C'mon Francisco, our class meets over here."

"My name is Frank," he said roughly, following me slowly.

He was quiet and respectful in class. I taught algebra and religion (quite a combination) and Frank's work was meticulous in each subject. His religion journal entries were quite honest. In reading them, I learned much about Frank and his environment.

For one, Frank rode the city bus from home to school each morning. Our school was in a fairly affluent area, while Frank lived in the central city, about 15 miles away. Each morning he left his house at 5 a.m. to catch the first of two buses to school.

Frank's enrollment at his last two schools had ended on unpleasant terms. He had been accused of stealing a boy's expensive athletic jacket at one school. More recently, his father had found him associating with older boys in his neighborhood who were thought to be gang members. In his journal, Frank explained both of these incidents and denied involvement in either of them.

One of his first questions was how he could make his First Communion. "My brothers have made theirs, but I never did," he said. Frank looked after the weaker kids in the class, especially for a boy named Arthur who was picked on frequently. "If you mess with Arthur, I'll mess with you," Frank told them.

For the first month or two, Frank was respectful to me. But, suddenly, his behavior changed. He began acting out in class and I caught him marking on a desk. I warned him, punished him, and finally tried to talk privately with him in a consoling and understanding manner, but to no avail. He would keep his head bowed, only occasionally glancing up with a sly kind of a smile. This habit of his only made me angrier.

I called Frank's father and explained to him what had happened. "Don't worry, sir," his father said. "I will take care of it." The next day Frank came early to school with his mother. "I am sorry for my behavior Mr. Doten," he whispered softly.

"Frank," I said, "I accept your apology but I would like you to be more respectful. And the way to do that is to look me in the eye." Frank glanced to his mother and then half-heartily looked up at me. "Thank you Frank," I told him.

When they left, Diana Guevarra, a student, commented, "Don't you know that in Hispanic families it is respectful to bow your head when you are addressing your elder? You are really confusing that poor kid."

▲ *Are you aware of how your students, like Frank, may have differing cultural needs and customs?*

Here was something else I didn't know. Frank's cultural and family background were certainly different from mine. And, yet, I was forcing him to conform to my ways of showing respect. Was I also doing the same with regard to his faith experience?

As a teacher and catechist, I wondered how I could learn about the many influences in my students' lives. How could I get a better understanding of what was helping **and** hindering their growth in faith?

Memo

What message can you find in the lyrics of "Cat's in the Cradle" on the first page of this chapter?

YOUR STORY

Students come to you from every type of family background. They are influenced by many different people and experiences. It is in this context that you begin your task as a catechist, aiding in the development of your students' faith. For a moment, think about the students you teach. Try to develop a background profile on some of the general family, peer, and social influences that affect their faith development. Describe these influences below.

1. How have your students helped you become a better catechist?

_____

_____

_____

2. Rank the spheres of influence in your students' faith development from most to least important (i.e. family, religion class, television, peers, parish, teachers, school, video games, sports).

_____

_____

_____

_____

3. What is one strategy you can use to incorporate family or ethnic customs and traditions into a student's faith development?

_____

_____

_____

4. As a catechist, how is your relationship with your students different than if you taught a subject other than religion?

_____

_____

_____

_____

The Life Situations in which Faith Grows

The story of Frank and your own reflections point out one of the ever-growing challenges for today's catechist. Students come from many different cultural and social environments. The faith environment you create in the short time you are with your students is but one of the many contexts in which your students live. The goal of the catechist is not to replace these environments but, rather, to understand them and know how they influence the lives of the students.

In shaping the faith environment, we can use the students' own life experiences as points of departure. Imagine what a seventh grade boy like Frank could share with his classmates about feelings of trust, betrayal, reconciliation, and anger from his experiences? What would it mean to attend different schools, hang with the fringe of a neighborhood gang, travel the city streets daily on a bus? Also, how could the other students in the group—most from a different area and culture—help Frank?

Faith is our response to a God who is always seeking us. So while we are limited by our circumstances, it is through those circumstances that we come to know God. Growing in faith does not happen in a vacuum. Rather, faith develops in the context of a very complex world. Literally all the circumstances of one's life have an influence on the way one's faith grows or fails to grow.

Pause a Moment . . .

• Describe how you have seen faith affected by your students' living environments.

• Make a list of ways that your students' experiences can be used as a starting point for a religious education class.

The Church Teaches

The *Catechism of the Catholic Church, (#166)* teaches that faith is a personal act that we make freely to the initiative of God. The Catechism recognizes that faith can never be an isolated act, for no one can believe alone. As believers, we have received faith from others with the obligation to hand it on to others out of love for Jesus. We are, thus, only a link in the great chain of believers. I am carried in faith by the faith of others, and, through my faith, I support others in theirs.

▲ *How can you help students to listen for God's call in everything they do, even play?*

General Influences on Students

As catechists, we are committed to the message of Jesus that we represent. We believe it is valuable and important, and that it makes a difference. We want to present the message clearly and accurately.

However, we also realize that the message is not complete unless it is lived by the students. Merely learning information is not enough. We are concerned with how students perceive the message, internalize it, and apply it to their thinking, talking, and behavior. Therefore, by considering what influences the students' attitudes and behaviors, we are not denying the importance of the message but, rather, finding more effective ways of communicating it, and thus affirming its ultimate importance.

The following factors are points a catechist might consider when trying to bring the message of Jesus to students from various backgrounds.

1. **Family.** Does the student experience his or her family as safe and stable? What is the student's relationship with his or her parents? To how many parents does the student relate—one, two, three, or even more? How does the family live out Christian values?

2. **Neighborhood.** Is the student's neighborhood safe? Does the neighborhood and community support or contradict the values promoted in your religion class? How are the students affected by gangs or by the abuse of alcohol and illegal drugs among family and peers?

3. **Peer group.** Are the values manifested in the student's peer group similar or contradictory to the values you present as a catechist? How much diversity and individuality does the student's peer group allow its members?

4. **Parish.** Is your parish supportive of youth and families? Are you confident and proud to invite your students to be members of your local parish? Does the parish make your students feel truly welcome and accepted?

5. **School.** What is the quality of the schools which your students attend? Can they receive a quality education if they desire? Is their school a wholesome place? Do the students feel safe there? What values do the students learn at school?

6. **Religion class.** Is your class a welcoming place for your students? Do they feel comfortable sharing both through general discussion and journal writing? Is the atmosphere conducive to shared prayer?

7. **Race and ethnicity.** Does each student feel accepted for his or her racial or ethnic background? Are ideas of God, Church, community, morality, life after death, and human relations understood and expressed differently in the ethnic group or culture of which the students are a part? Is magic or superstition a factor in the students' daily lives? Do they feel comfortable communicating in English?

8. **Media.** What values are communicated in the music your students prefer? What are some of the programs that your students watch? What are the values extolled in these shows? How are they influenced by advertising?

Notes

9. **Local, National, and International Community.** What is the atmosphere in the students' local community? Do they have a sense of ownership of it? On a national level, is their patriotism balanced? Do they sense that their national government is sensitive to human rights, to justice at home and around the world? Are they concerned about how international military action could involve a family member? Do they live in fear of terrorism? Are they aware of global hunger? How do they feel about the unequal distribution of the world's resources?

10. **Social class.** Is "class" or social standing considered a factor that makes one superior or inferior? Is education valued? Do the perceived social classes from which your students come mingle in school, community, or social activities? Do the members of different social classes trust or fear one another? How do students relate to material possessions? Are they limited by their poverty?

More about Social Development

Psychoanalyst Erik Erikson's theory of social and emotional development centers on these stages:

- **Stage 1: Infancy—Trust vs. Mistrust.** In the first year of life, one of a child's main tasks is to develop trust.

- **Stage 2: Early Childhood—Autonomy vs. Shame and Doubt.** During the second and third years of life, the child will develop a sense of autonomy provided that he or she is encouraged to try new things.

- **Stage 3: Childhood—Initiative vs. Guilt.** During the fourth and fifth years, physical capacities develop to the point where the child can initiate play activities rather than merely following other children.

- **Stage 4: Later Childhood—Industry vs. Inferiority.** During the early school years, children develop a new sense of industry that is reinforced through praise and reward.

- **Stage 5: Adolescence—Identity vs. Role Confusion.** During adolescence, people are primarily concerned with the question of who they are.

- **Stage 6: Young Adulthood—Intimacy vs. Isolation.** The crisis that confronts the young adult comes from the efforts to share with, and care about, another person.

- **Stage 7: Middle Age—Generativity vs. Self-Absorption.** In middle age, a person's satisfaction is likely to come from helping others.

- **Stage 8: Advanced Age—Integrity vs. Despair.** People who feel that they have made a contribution to others during their lives have feelings of self-acceptance and integrity.

Pause a Moment...

- How can these ten issues influence one's experience of faith?
- Which of the general influences mentioned above have you least considered?
- Has considering any of these general influences given you a better understanding of a particular student's attitudes or behavior?

God's Relentless Call

In the unlikeliness of our present surroundings, we are called to form a relationship with God. Only after first hearing God's call can a life of faith eventually be lived. The relentlessness of God's call is evidenced in the Scriptures. For example:

- Abandoned to the solitude of the desert, Moses heard God's voice calling out from a bush. "Come, now! I will send you to Pharaoh to lead My people, the Israelites, out of Egypt" *(Exodus 3:10).*

- The prophet Samuel was awakened by God's voice calling to him over and over in his sleep. Finally, Samuel, answered: "Speak, for Your servant is listening" *(1 Samuel 3:10).*

- Jeremiah refused to heed God's call to speak words of warning to the people. "Ah, Lord God! I know not how to speak; I am too young." The Lord responded: "Say not, 'I am too young.' To whomever I send you, you shall go; whatever I command you, you shall speak. Have no fear before them because I am with you to deliver you" *(Jeremiah 1:6-8).*

Where will your students hear God's voice calling to them? Will it be in the surroundings of family, either healthy or broken, or through friends and peers? Will they hear God's call to positions of leadership so that justice may prevail?

A successful catechist is one who reminds the students that God is always with them, present in their everyday surroundings. This catechist recognizes that God calls through the values and images of our culture, not in spite of them. This catechist uses what culture offers and helps students hear God's call in all things, so that they may answer: "Here I am, send me!" *(Isaiah 6:8).*

Pause a Moment . . .

- Describe to a partner your experience of God touching a student experiencing difficulty.

- Develop a strategy for helping students discover God's presence in their everyday experiences.

▲ *What are some of the negative influences in your students' lives?*

▲ *How can you build on the positive influences in your students' lives?*

Ranking and Comparing the Influences

Which of the following general influences on faith are most important in the lives of your students? In the first column on the chart below, rank them in the order of importance from 1 to 10. Next, share your rankings with two other catechists (preferably catechists who work with students of a different age than you do). Write their rankings in the second and third columns. What similarities and differences are found in the rankings?

General Influences	My Ranking	Catechist 1	Catechist 2
Family			
Neighborhood			
Peer group			
Parish			
School			
Religion class			
Race and ethnicity			
Media			
Community			
Social class			

1. Which influence did you rank most important? Which influence did you rank least important? Why?

_____

_____

_____

2. What did you learn by comparing your rankings with those of other catechists?

_____

_____

_____

$\mathcal{P}$art III $\mathcal{D}$iscovery

The Origins of Your Students' Faith

Evaluating influences and how they affect your students is an ongoing and important task. The effect the family has on a child's image of God and his or her overall religious development cannot be discounted.

John Westerhoff in *Will Our Children Have Faith?* explains that the first of three levels of faith is experiential; that is, young children take on the faith of those around them. Needless to say, great importance is attached to the religious example exhibited to children, especially in their first years of life.

As Pope John Paul II wrote,

> *"By virtue of their ministry of educating, parents are, through the witness of their lives, the first heralds of the Gospel for their children. Furthermore, by praying with their children, by reading the Word of God with them and by introducing them deeply through Christian initiation into the Body of Christ—both the eucharistic and ecclesial body—they become fully parents, in that they are begetters not only of bodily life but also of the life that through the Spirit's renewal flows from the cross and resurrection of Christ"* (Familiaris Consortio, #39).

A family can be a powerful experience of personal acceptance and basic religious and moral values upon which a religious education program can build. Or, the family can be violent, degrading, or morally bankrupt, defeating the best attempts of religious educators.

The *Catechism of the Catholic Church, #2225* stresses the cooperation between parents and catechists in the religious education of children. The parent's role is understood as one of faith initiator, not as formal teacher holding classes in the home. Parents should initiate their children into the mysteries of faith.

Catechists can only complement and build on what happens at home. This is one of the first lessons a catechist must understand. Unfortunately, many children live in families where religious cultures and traditions are no longer practiced. Many Catholic families no longer attend church regularly. Some parents believe that religion is a subject that is to be taught and can be put off until a child is older. Many of the children whom you teach will come to you from this type of non-experience of religion in the family.

$\mathcal{N}$otes

$\mathcal{P}$ause a $\mathcal{M}$oment . . .

- From your own experience, describe, in writing, the amount of involvement you can expect from parents. Share your thoughts with a partner.

- Discuss how you can be more aware of the different family backgrounds of your students as you create a welcoming class environment.

- How can you work in partnership with parents in the religious education of their children?

Problems within the Family

What if your students come from a family where the parents are constantly arguing with one another and not providing the proper social, emotional, and religious support for their children?

1. Encourage your students to not blame themselves or assume responsibility for their parents' problems.

2. Direct students to someone who is trained to help them with their personal problems.

3. Encourage students to accept their families as they are.

4. Stay in touch with the students and their home situation.

5. In some situations, students will show signs of abuse. Find out the diocesan policy for handling these situations. Immediately report these cases to your DRE or principal.

Other Influences

The impact of the student's life situation on his or her growth in faith is illustrated most vividly in the Parable of the Sower *(Matthew 13:1–23, Mark 4:1–20 or Luke 8:4–15)*. The seed is always the same. But the places it falls (the context, the life situation) vary widely and so do the results.

Often any one of these general influences can have both a positive and negative effect at the same time. For example, the various households of a neighborhood may be supportive of values such as family, private property, even religious education. On the other hand, many households in that same neighborhood could be quietly influencing their children to adopt materialistic values by continually providing them with the latest style of clothes, the most expensive athletic shoes, and every new toy that appears on the market. All the children in the neighborhood will be affected by this, even those children from households that prize or can afford only a simple lifestyle.

All these influences are present in your students in some way. These influences may be helping your students to connect with, agree with, or perceive the point you are teaching. Or, these influences may be interfering with, contradicting, or clouding your students' understanding and acceptance of the points you are presenting.

Pause a Moment . . .

- Describe, in writing, the general lessons your students are learning from their neighborhoods, their schools, and the media.

- How can you build on the influences in your students' lives—positive and negative—in developing your lessons? Discuss your thoughts on these questions in a small group.

Scripture Background

In first-century Palestine, the sower walked over the fields to plant seeds. The fields were bare since the last harvest, except for a growth of thorns and footpaths. The thorns and other weeds were allowed to grow with the crop. Only after the crop had grown tall was the unedible growth removed and destroyed.

The Indispensable Element

Having sensitivity to the students' life situation is an indispensable element of the teaching process. It is an approach that Jesus himself used with great success. Jesus was clearly aware of the life situation of the people He addressed. In the story of the woman at the well *(John 4:4–42)*, Jesus surprised the Samaritan woman when he told her he knew her life story. Jesus' sensitivity to her situation prompted her conversion.

Later, Saint Paul, the Apostle to the Gentiles, followed Jesus' example in meeting people where they were by saying that he became all things to all people for the sake of the Gospel:

> *"Although I am free in regard to all, I have made myself a slave to all so as to win over as many as possible. To the Jews I became like a Jew to win over Jews; to those under the law I became like one under the law—though I myself am not under the law—to win over those under the law. To those outside the law I became like one outside the law—though I am not outside God's law but within the law of Christ—to win over those outside the law. To the weak I became weak, to win over the weak. I have become all things to all, to save at least some. All this I do for the sake of the Gospel, so that I too may have a share in it"* (1 Corinthians 9:19–23).

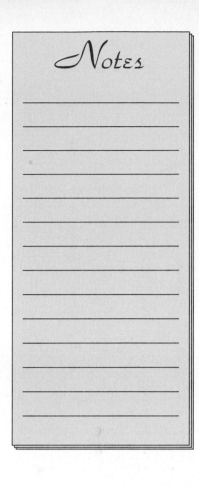

Notes

▲ *The public media, especially television, have a powerful influence over children and their behavior.*

Remote and Proximate Influences

While the general aspects of a person's life are always an influencing factor, they are not necessarily on one's mind or always having an immediate effect. For instance, the fact that a person has no father or comes from a poor family may not affect him or her at a given moment in your religion class. These are remote influences. However, proximate or immediate influences do have an impact on a person in the present moment. For example, a fight that took place just before class or the fact that a student had no sleep the night before will have an influence on how he or she receives the message you are communicating.

The following list specifies some immediate or proximate influences:

1. **Family.** A student may have just experienced the giving or receiving of forgiveness with a parent, brother, or sister. Or the student may have had a major disagreement with a family member.

2. **Physical or mental impairments.** Problems such as poor vision, the inability to concentrate, constant fatigue, low learning ability, and a lack of a balanced diet always have an immediate effect on how a student participates in your class.

3. **Classroom atmosphere.** You may be a thorough, well-prepared, creative, and dynamic catechist, but if your class setting is dirty, dreary, poorly lighted, too hot or cold, too small or large, or lacking the proper furniture, it will be difficult for your students to respond with interest and excitement. This is as true for adults as it is for young children.

4. **Experiences just prior to class.** A good or bad day at school or home will still be affecting a student's feelings. Seventh graders who have spent their day constantly avoiding the class bullies may have difficulty concentrating on your lesson. The effects of a physical or verbal fight will still be present. Also, pleasant experiences such as an important ball-game or an interesting field trip will consume the students' attention.

5. **Timing.** How would you describe the difference in your own effectiveness on the job between the morning and afternoon hours? Studies show that students (and teachers) concentrate on a lesson and study material better in the early morning than after lunch. Also, the length of the class period itself will affect your students' ability to learn.

6. **Catechist's mood.** How you feel emotionally or physically will affect the influence you have on your students. Interestingly, this factor may work in different ways than you might suspect. For example, a first-year teacher who was experiencing problems maintaining order in his classroom found that on the days that he had a slight cold or was feeling tired, the students generally behaved better. The students clearly understood his mood and adjusted their behavior to suit it. From then on, he made a special effort to communicate clearly to the students his mood and subsequent expectations to the students. Whether you are generally optimistic or pessimistic, trusting or suspicious will have an impact on your students' behavior.

▲ *Teenagers greatly desire independence, but they also still crave the attention and support of their parents and other adults.*

7. **Weather.** Bad storms, extreme heat or cold, bright or dreary days all have an effect on your students.

Write your answers to the following questions and share them with a fellow catechist.

1. What are some things you can do to respond to the negative influences in your students' lives?

_____

_____

2. What can you do to enhance the positive influences in your students' lives?

_____

_____

Additional Influences

Use these questions and approaches to learn more about what influences the faith development of your students:

Primary students (grades K-3). Television has a disproportionate influence on the lives of children at this age. Determine the popular Saturday morning television programs your students watch. If possible, videotape the programs and show them in class. Then elicit responses from the children on the following issues: (1) What are the relationships between the characters? Do they mainly help each other or hurt each other? (2) Have the students keep count on a piece of paper each violent act they see in the episode. Ask them to compare their own behavior to the behavior they witnessed in the episode. (3) How does the story end? Point out that in our own lives simple solutions to problems we experience don't exist.

Intermediate students (grades 4-6) and the playground. Recess and life on the school playground is important for children of this age. Competitive sports are often the norm for most boys and girls, with some students who wish to play left off teams and out of games. Boys and girls who themselves have low self-esteem may heap verbal and physical abuse on those they perceive as weaker.

On a more positive note, friendships are formed on the playground. Students who are quiet in the classroom may be the most outgoing on the playground. The freedom of unsupervised play is often the happiest time in the lives of children.

Here are some suggestions for learning more about your students:

1. Observe them at play.

2. Attend your students' extracurricular activities.

3. Have the students write about their likes and dislikes of recess and free play. Try to read between the lines to uncover what is primarily influencing each person in those settings.

4. Show an episode of the video series, "McGee and Me." Ask your students to consider a discussion such as presented there.

Junior high students (grades 7–8). A common activity for pre-adolescents is the trip to the mall with a group of friends. Issues of acceptance

Notes

among peers, independence, and a growing understanding of consumerism often arise in these settings. You may wish to:

1. Arrange an outing to the local shopping mall. If possible, plan a mall version of a scavenger hunt in cooperation with the mall merchants. Students work together in small groups to find the answers to clues you provide to reach a certain finish point. Use this activity as a basis for a follow-up discussion on the influence that "hanging out at the mall" has on their lives.

2. Take a trip to the mall on your own during after-school hours. Observe the dress, behavior, and types of junior high students you find there.

3. Ask the students to discuss the following issues in relation to their own experience: stealing, the last two movies they attended, purchasing name brand items, influences of high school-aged students, and meeting with friends of the opposite sex.

4. Ask them to explain how they would feel if they had to select their next pair of athletic shoes by drawing a brand name out of a hat.

High school students (grades 9–12). There are, of course, many influences in the lives of high school students. Have them analyze the lyrics of a popular song and ask if they and their friends agree with the song's message. Examining the kinds of afterschool work and the importance of the work in your students' lives can help you understand their vocational plans, need for money, and the effort they give in other areas of their lives (schoolwork, relationships, religion, for example). You may wish to have a career day in class where the students can share their dreams for the future and their current work experiences. Also, have the students write or discuss what they have learned from after-school work about relationships with employers, responsibility, or the need to plan and train for future careers and vocations.

Pause a Moment . . .

• List some of the other influences on the students you teach. How can you learn more about your students from the things that influence them?

• Share with a fellow catechist a personal strategy that you have used to key into the things that influence your students outside of the classroom.

▲ *High school age students have begun to consider the broad horizons that are their future. How can you link their future plans to the Gospel message?*

▲ *Who have been the sowers who planted God's Word in your heart?*

Prayer Response

The Parable of the Sower: A Reflection. As you read the words of the Parable of the Sower from the Gospel according to Luke, recall those sowers who have planted God's Word in your own heart. Maybe it was your grandmother who planted a garden with you and taught you about the goodness of God's abundance or a friend whose life was filled with suffering, yet remained positive and hopeful. Was there someone special who made God's Word come alive for you? Remember your sponsors and relatives who supported you as you prepared for the sacraments, and the priests and religious who shaped your growing faith. Remember especially your parents, who gave you both physical life and life in the Spirit.

1. Who are some of the sowers in your life?

_____

2. What is your fondest memory of a sower and how he or she nurtured your faith?

_____

3. Like the birds who ate the seed, who are the people or circumstances which seek to snatch away our faith?

_____

4. The rocky soil suggests an unwillingness on our part to respond to God's Word. What are some distractions that keep you from allowing God's Word to take root in your life? What are the distractions for your students?

_____

5. Imagine a garden overgrown with thorns. The thorns choke out everything that was sown. What are the thorns in your life? What have you allowed to choke off your relationship with God? What are some thorns in the lives of your students?

_____

6. Seeds need nourishment: food, water, sunlight. What can you do to help God's Word take deep root in your life? In the lives of your students?

_____

The New Commandment

When a large crowd gathered, with people from one town after another journeying to him, he spoke in parable. "A sower went out to sow his seed. And as he sowed, some seed fell on the path and was trampled, and the birds of the sky ate it up. Some seed fell on rocky ground, and when it grew, it withered for lack of moisture. Some seed fell among thorns, and the thorns grew with it and choked it. And some seed fell on good soil, and when it grew, it produced fruit a hundredfold." After saying this, he called out, "Whoever has ears to hear ought to hear."

(Luke 8:4-8).

Notes

_____

_____

_____

_____

_____

_____

_____

_____

_____

_____

Your Students

Consider the proximate influences listed in this section and others that you know have an effect on your students. List those proximate influences (they can be positive or negative) and describe the effect each has on your students.

Proximate Influences	Effect
_____	_____
_____	_____
_____	_____

- What are your students generally like when they first arrive at class?

- Give an example of a time when you took into consideration a proximate influence on your students. Describe the strategy you used.

- In light of what I have learned about the many influences on a person's development in faith, I want to keep the following considerations in mind for the next time I meet with my students.

_____

_____

BIBLIOGRAPHY

Coles, Robert. *The Spiritual Life of Children.* Boston: Houghton Mifflin, 1990.

Center for Media and Values. *Catholic Connections to Media Literacy.* Los Angeles. Multi-media Kit, 1992.

Ekstrom, Reynolds R., editor. *Media and Culture.* New Rochelle, New York: Don Bosco Multimedia, 1992.

Franciscan Communications. *The Heart to Heart Collection.*

Maternach, Janaan and Pfeifer, Carl J. *Creative Catechist.* West Mystic, Connecticut: Twenty-Third Publications, 1991. See Chapter 6, "Natural Signs: Life and Culture."

National Conference of Catholic Bishops. Chapter I, Chapter II, and Chapter VIII, in *Sharing the Light of Faith.* Washington, DC: USCC Publications, 1979.

Potvin, Raymond H., and Hoge, Dean R. *Religion and American Youth.* Washington, DC: USCC Publications, 1976.

Ratliff, Donald, editor. *Handbook of Children's Religious Education.* Birmingham: Religious Education Press, 1992.

Roberto, John, editor. *Guide to Understanding Youth.* New Rochelle, New York: Don Bosco Multimedia, 1991. Especially Chapter 6, "Understanding Youth Culture."

Westerhoff, John. *Will Our Children Have Faith?* New York: Seabury Press, 1976.

Nihil Obstat
The Reverend Robert D. Lunsford, M. A.

Imprimatur
The Most Reverend Kenneth J. Povish, D. D.
Bishop of Lansing
June 24, 1993

The *Nihil Obstat* and *Imprimatur* are official declarations that a book or pamphlet is free of doctrinal or moral error. No implication is contained therein that those who have granted the *Nihil Obstat* and *Imprimatur* agree with the contents, opinions, or statements expressed.

Scripture passages are taken from *The New American Bible with Revised New Testament,* copyright © 1988 by the Confraternity of Christian Doctrine, Washington, D.C. All rights reserved.

Copyright © 1994 by the Glencoe Division of Macmillan/McGraw-Hill School Publishing Company. All rights reserved. Except as permitted under the United States Copyright Act, no part of this publication may be reproduced or distributed in any form or by any means, or stored in a database or retrieval system, without the prior written permission of the publisher.

This chapter may be ordered separately using the following ISBN number.

Send all inquiries to:
BENZIGER PUBLISHING COMPANY
15319 Chatsworth Street
P.O. Box 9609
Mission Hills, California 91346-9609

Second Edition

ISBN 0-02-651195-9

Printed in the United States of America.

1 2 3 4 5 6 7 8 9 BAW 97 96 95 94 93

Benziger

Responding to Your Students as Persons

The question remains, though: what kind or how much psychology do you need to be an effective catechist? My answer is quite simple: enough to help you understand your students, and to help them understand themselves. Note the stress is on understanding, not on problem solving. You're not in the business of problem solving; but if you can aid self-understanding, the student will have a precious tool for solving problems and making decisions. Moreover, he or she will be in a better position to understand and live our Christian faith.

Father Martin Pable, "Who Needs Psychology?"

In this chapter you will:

- Determine the significance of various stages of personality development in teaching religion.
- Apply age level teaching suggestions through specific lessons and activities.
- Adapt case studies of lessons to the needs of your students.

Second Edition

Copyright © Glencoe, Macmillan/McGraw-Hill

Special Visitors

What a surprise! Just as I finished greeting my kindergarten and preschool catechists, who should appear but Grandpa Edward and Grandma Lucy. They had driven to Denver from their home in Colorado Springs, about 150 miles round trip, to visit me, their oldest granddaughter, at their former parish, Saint Mark's.

Of course Sunday morning is my busiest of days, when every kid from four to eighteen years old, catechists, helpers, musicians, and parents want me. Grandma, the catechism teacher from the 1950s, and Grandpa, a parish council founder, had picked a difficult time for a tour.

I decided to go with the flow. "Follow me," I said. "Our first stop is the basement." It wasn't really the basement, just the ground floor classrooms. It was there that the preschool and kindergarten classes met with certified catechists Nancy, Brenda, Denise, and Pam. Grandma poked her head inside the room for four-year-olds, where Nancy and Brenda's kids had cutouts of the sun fastened around their heads. They were pantomiming the words to a song.

"Are those halos they're wearing?" Grandpa wanted to know.

Brenda overheard. "Oh, no. Our lesson today is about light and darkness. Don't you think they make darling little sunshines?"

"Uh, sure," said Grandpa. Then turning to me, he whispered: "Sheila, this is a big parish. I only count eight children in this class."

"That's the maximum class size for children this age. We have another class for four-year-olds that meets during the next Mass," I explained.

Meanwhile, Grandma came back from the kindergarten group across the way. "Anything interesting?" I wanted to know.

"The teachers had the children making up their own prayers," she said. "Isn't this the age when they should be learning and memorizing traditional prayers?"

"No, Grandma. Spontaneous prayer is the best way for children of this age—and maybe for all of us—to pray," I said.

Grandma and Grandpa were moving on—without me it seemed. "Hey, you guys, over here," I motioned.

"Where are those kids going?" Grandpa wanted to know. Boom boxes blared. Eighth grader Frankie Kane approached us and asked me if I could tie the bandanna that held together his pony tail. Altogether, about 25 seventh and eighth graders piled into several minivans along with parents, catechists, and the senior high students acting as helpers and chaperones.

"They're off to the lake," I said.

"Is that all they do for religious education?" asked Grandpa.

"No, Grandpa. They have already been to Mass at 8 a.m. where they lector, usher, and serve as greeters. Then they eat breakfast together and discuss the Scripture readings they just heard. Now they will play together for the rest of the day."

"What I remember about eighth grade religion was Mr. Broglio, hard wooden desks, and the Baltimore Catechism."

Grandma added, "And Latin."

"Right, and Latin," said Grandpa.

"This junior high group meets every other week," I told them. "We've found that a combination of formal and informal activities works well. Besides, trips to the lake build a great spirit!"

"By the way," I added, "Did you see Kerry, Bill, Rebecca, Ross, and Dana? Those were those bigger-looking teens or smaller-looking adults—whatever you prefer. They're in our second year Confirmation class. Working with the junior high program is a Confirmation service project. But I really think they like going on trips to the lake, roller-skating, bike riding, and skiing just as much as the other kids."

Just then Laura Kiedrowski passed by on her way to Mass. I could tell that something was on her mind too. She handed me a copy of her school newspaper, pointing to an article with her byline. I glanced at the article, then showed it to Grandma. "Did that girl write this?" she asked.

I nodded. It was a well-written, moving editorial on the need for prayer in public schools—our topic at the last Confirmation meeting. "Laura comes to Confirmation class, too," I said. "She's not sure yet if she wants to be confirmed, but she does come. And she brings lots of non-Catholic friends!"

"These programs you sponsor are sure interesting," Grandpa admitted. "I was just wondering. . . .

"Edward," Grandma interrupted, "if we don't get moving we are going to be late for Mass."

I let out a noticeable sigh. Then I realized that when Grandma and Grandpa attended the 10:30 Children's Liturgy and saw the kids leave with their teachers for the Liturgy of the Word they would have practically seen or heard about every child-centered religion program at Saint Mark's. All in a one hour tour! I needed a break.

▲ *Grandma and Grandpa were encouraged that young children still learned the sign of the cross.*

▲ *Special outings and field trips add interest to formal programs.*

Program Characteristics

The report, *A Hopeful Horizon,* published in 1993 by the National Catholic Educational Association, determined that the majority of the parish religious education programs which they studied:

- Have a full-time, paid director of religious education.
- Have written goals for the catechetical program.
- Have a budget for catechetical programs.
- Emphasize adult religious education programs.
- Experience a high degree of diocesan support for catechists.
- Share planning and coordination with a lay group; e.g., parish council, or religious education board.
- Have a significant number of support volunteers who are not catechists.
- Recruit catechists continually.
- Average about one catechist for each ten active participants.
- Provide for the training of catechists.
- Have access to a range of audiovisual resources.
- Offer service projects for junior and senior high school youth.

YOUR STORY

After Grandpa Edward and Grandma Lucy went to 10:30 Mass, they headed off to find their car in the crowded church parking lot. Just then, Grandma spots . . . YOU!

"Why, excuse me, weren't you the catechist I saw today on my tour?"

"Of course it is, Lucy!" Grandpa chimes in.

You are asked to explain the modern catechetical approach for the children you teach. "Why do you choose the activities that you do?" they want to know. "Do the children today seem interested in religion? What has been your greatest success as a catechist? Your greatest failure?"

Grandpa and Grandma want to know it all! What do you tell them? Write some of your answers and explanations to their questions on the lines below. If you wish, you can write your story in the form of a role-play.

_____

_____

_____

_____

_____

_____

_____

_____

_____

_____

_____

_____

_____

ℐart II ℳessage

Stages of Personality Development

To understand why parish catechetical programs differ for every level from preschool to adult is to understand something about the meaning and development of the human person. As you explore the various stages and implications of personality development, it is important to consider a few definitions at the beginning. *Person* will be used to refer to a human being. *Personality* will refer to the sum total of an individual's characteristics, an integrated group of emotional trends, behaviors, and tendencies.

Though the foundation of one's personality is basically formed by the time he or she reaches kindergarten (individuals usually are confident, shy, outspoken, or personable by that age), there are several typical personality characteristics that develop at each age level from birth to late adulthood. This section will look at these developments and how they impact you, the catechist.

Because the life of faith is related to human growth, it, too, passes through stages of development. Religious education is meant to give direction and meaning at each stage of human development and lead ultimately to patterning the values of Jesus in one's life. One of the catechetical developments following the Second Vatican Council was the recognition that Revelation takes place at the learner's or hearer's capacity to receive it. The behavioral sciences can help us to understand our students whose faith is developing, but they cannot cause faith or even growth in faith. Neither can the catechist. Faith is a gift from God. Different people possess aspects of God's gift of faith to varying degrees.

ℳεmo

What characteristics do you notice most in the students you teach?

Personality Characteristics and Faith Development Implications

Take a close look at the various stages. Underline the parts that seem especially significant to you. Look for typical patterns in personality development according to the characteristics that are listed. You may be especially interested in the age level you teach, but it will be helpful to pay close attention to the levels immediately before and after your students.

Infancy and Early Childhood

From birth to age five, important psychological foundations are laid. These influence the ability of the person to successfully begin three lifelong tasks necessary for maturity: (1) accepting oneself, (2) relating with others, and (3) responding to one's environment.

People who are full of self-doubt or lack self-esteem have difficulty establishing stable relationships. People who have not experienced trust in their initial relationships usually have trouble relating with others in confidence.

Healthy personal growth takes place in a positive nurturing environment, often in the immediate family. Through the experience of love and acceptance, youths will learn to accept who they are. If the child experiences consistent,

In the Last Supper discourse from the Gospel of John, Jesus' words hint at his understanding of human development and its affect on learning. Here are some other examples of Jesus' words from the Gospels that reflect this understanding.

"I have more to tell you, but you cannot bear it now"

(John 16:12).

"I have told you this in figures of speech. The hour is coming when I will no longer speak to you in figures but I will tell you clearly about the Father"

(John 16:25).

dependable relationships, he or she will show an ability to relate to others with confidence. If the child has a sense of personal freedom and is encouraged to be expressive and creative, that child will approach his or her environment with confidence. He or she will not always need to be directed.

Some implications for the catechist are:

1. Praise is important for all children, especially at this age. Self-confidence, independence, and responsibility develop through praise received from an adult or trusted other. Without self-esteem, a person will have difficulty believing that others, including God, could really care. How do you use praise in your catechesis?

2. Preschoolers model adult behavior. Infants and young children primarily experience God's love through their parents. They pattern their behavior on what they see adults do. How can you model this positive behavior for them?

3. Preschool children are keenly aware of the environment outside of their home. Three year olds—as the catechist in the opening story pointed out—are able to find God's presence in all of nature. How do you encourage initiative and creativity?

Childhood

Children from ages six to ten develop emotionally through satisfactory relationships with a widening circle of people. The person's world expands beyond the immediate family. By nine or ten, the typical child learns to control his or her emotions most of the time. The periods of instability in emotional behavior that marked the younger years have likely waned.

The three tasks described for infancy and early childhood undergo significant development at this age. Children become aware of specific talents they possess or lack. Innocent trust gives way to a qualified trust, excluding some people and situations. They begin to recognize that their personal freedom is modified by the rights and freedom of others.

Implications for the catechist include:

1. The child is now able to connect his or her life experiences with the teachings and values of Jesus.

2. Through their emotional growth, children can begin to move away from their natural selfishness; sharing and helping makes a great deal more sense to them now.

3. Because significant changes are occurring in the students' ability to learn and understand, certain prayer formulas become understandable. The deeper meaning of stories, such as the parables of Jesus, can now be examined.

4. Children at this age develop keen senses of justice and fairness. What you do for one, they expect you to do for all.

Preadolescence and Puberty

The years from ten to thirteen are marked by rapid changes. Many of these changes are physical, and have to do with a person's emerging sexuality. Such changes, and the accompanying heightened sexual awareness, have a direct bearing on how the students perceive other people and relate to them. According to the National Catechetical Directory, boys and girls of this age "need to accept themselves precisely as male or female and to acquire a whole new way of relating to others" (*NCD, #179*).

As young people "try on" these changes, they may be unsure of the "fit." This uncertainty is within them. However, they may presume that other people are as uncomfortable with them as they are with themselves. They may begin to doubt others' acceptance of them: "I feel so dumb. I'm the only one with braces. No one will want to be seen with me."

As a catechist you will need to consider:

1. The students' expanding personal freedom. With the increased responsibility for directing one's actions comes an increased readiness to accept the consequences of those actions. Now, more than ever, the person's interests extend beyond the home to one's peer group.

2. Hero worship. The choice of heroes, however, is not limited to the latest media star or fad. Many preadolescents list such people as an older sibling, a coach, or a youth leader as heroes.

3. Prayer and service to others become more meaningful to these young people.

4. The question of identity. Students at this age have multiple identities and they are not always able to use the appropriate one in a given situation. They are influenced greatly by their peer groups.

Adolescence

In adolescence, physical growth is rapid and uneven. Girls, on the average, start maturing physically between the ages of 11 and 13. Boys generally mature between the ages of 12 and 16. During this time, secondary sex characteristics develop in both sexes.

The transition from childhood to adulthood can be difficult. The self-confidence, relationship skills, individuality, and understanding of reality gained in childhood can seem insufficient, with little at hand to replace them.

With all of these uncertainties, many adolescents develop a profound lack of self-confidence. The problem is magnified as they try to sort out their growing perception of life's complexity and ambiguity. The adolescent's turmoil and self-doubt are often expressed in external symptoms such as boredom, frustration, sharp changes in mood, withdrawal, rebellion, and apathy towards religion.

During this time, abstract thinking skills also develop. Adolescents develop the ability to recognize another's point of view and better evaluate problems. Emotionally, adolescents grow more caring; that is, they recognize the need to reach out to others and the need to take greater responsibility for the world around them. At this age they also become capable of developing a more personal image and relationship with God.

For an adolescent, social growth is also very important. Some of the major developmental tasks associated with this are: (1) forming more mature relationships with peers of both sexes, (2) accepting one's maturing self, (3) achieving emotional independence from parents and other adults, (4) preparing for career and vocation, and (5) the ability to use values as a guide for behavior.

Intellectual Development

Swiss psychologist Jean Piaget offered four stages of normal intellectual development:
- In the sensory-motor stage, infants learn through their senses and express themselves by their actions.
- During preschool and early school years, children learn by trial and error.
- Between the ages of 7 and 11, children start concrete thinking. They see events from different viewpoints, develop problem-solving skills, and handle simple reasoning.
- Between the ages of 12 and 18, formal thinking develops—complex reasoning, problem solving, connecting ideas and events, questioning, and forming beliefs and values.

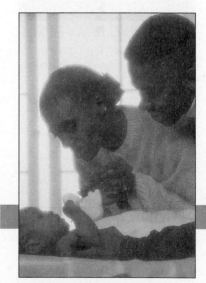

▲ *Children learn important lessons in infancy (e.g. how to trust) that will shape their later attitudes and behavior.*

During these years, adolescents are attempting to formulate some direction and purpose for themselves. For this reason, attention should be given to presenting the rational basis for faith—life does have meaning; faith can give direction; it is reasonable to hope. Many adolescents have an increasing ability to respond to life with a maturing faith. There is a tendency for their prayer to become more personal and reflective. They also now begin to consider vocational choices.

Pause a Moment . . .

- How do adolescents demonstrate a lack of self-confidence? What are some experiences that can help to improve their self-confidence?

- What are limits you would place on an adolescent's desire to seek independence? How could you encourage the desire for positive independence?

- Suggest a project or activity to foster an awareness of Christian values and vocational choices.

Stages in Adulthood

▲ *At every age, parents still play a vital role in the faith of their children. The Church calls parents the "primary" catechist.*

We live in a time of greatly increased life expectancy. Over 80 percent of today's newborns are expected to live beyond age 60. In 1830, only 30 percent of babies could expect to live that long. Because of this increase, the characteristics and implications of stages of adulthood have taken on greater significance. Here is an overview of three stages of adulthood.

Early Adulthood

The ages from eighteen to about thirty-five are typically classified as early adulthood, even though not everyone in this stage has necessarily reached psychological, emotional, or spiritual maturity. Young adults may be single, married, parents, separated, divorced, or widowed.

During this period, life decisions such as vocation, career, selection of a marriage partner, and personal goals are made. A prolonged unwillingness to make any life choices prevents one's continued growth and is probably a sign that, regardless of age, the person is still at an earlier stage of maturity.

Many young adults break their ties with organized religion, although a significant number of them do return to the practice of their faith later in life. They usually have had profound personal reasons for stopping the practice of their faith and later returning to it. Parish-based programs that welcome returning Catholics to active participation in the Church are very effective.

Middle Adulthood

Usually, a person enters adulthood with great optimism, enthusiasm, and self-confidence. One's ideals are clear, high goals have been set, there is much ambition, and challenges are eagerly accepted.

But at some point, the individual often experiences a "crisis of limits." Careers seem to have reached a deadend, a marriage may break up, health problems surface. A spiritual crisis is also likely. Adults ask, "What is the meaning and purpose of my life? What will happen to me when I die?" An experience of failure or personal weakness can cause a loss of self-esteem. Ideals suffer under such harsh reality.

People can learn to accept and understand these experiences and changes. They can learn to negotiate their original ideals in light of their present reality. The ability to accept what life offers during middle adulthood positively indicates a movement toward a new level of maturity. From acceptance it is now possible to deepen one's relationship with God and with others. Some people are willing and able to be at God's disposal to reach out to and serve the needs of others.

Late Adulthood

As people mature, their increased knowledge and acceptance of self makes it possible for them to enter into self-giving relationships with others. They are often capable of higher levels of personal freedom and don't feel as limited as they once did by what others think. These can be the most creative and fruitful years of a person's life. Older adults are an extremely valuable resource in our faith communities. Unfortunately, they (and their needs) are often overlooked. They seldom are asked to share their wisdom and unique experience of faith with the parish.

Pause a Moment . . .

- Discuss with a partner how the Church can better reach out and meet the needs of adults in their various stages of development.

- In a few sentences, describe how Edward and Lucy, the grandparents from the opening story, might contribute to the parish's religious education program.

YOUR VIEW

Which of the above characteristics best describe your students?

_____

_____

_____

_____

_____

_____

_____

What characteristics would you add to the list for your students?

_____

_____

_____

_____

_____

Notes

Memo

How can you incorporate play into your lesson planning?

Suggestions for Catechists

As a catechist, you want to use skillfully the knowledge about your students' personality and faith development so that you are most helpful to their growth as Christians. The following section specifies the personality characteristics for each grade level and offers practical suggestions for successfully communicating the Good News to your students.

It is not possible in the present space to fully develop these stages. You will find additional useful information about the psychological development of your students and appropriate teaching methods in the introduction or resource section of your grade level's teacher's manual. What is provided here will help you understand the basics for the students you teach.

Preschool-Kindergarten Characteristics

Three-, four- and five-year-olds view everything in relationship to themselves. These children do not understand the concept of shared rights or shared points of view; they believe that everything is as they see it. Three-, four-, and five-year-olds have a limited understanding of such mature concepts as right or wrong, good or bad. Something is wrong only if one is caught. Something is right if it satisfies a need; it is not right if the satisfaction is delayed.

Here are teaching suggestions to use with preschool and kindergarten students. How might these suggestions be applied through specific lessons or activities?

*   Play is the most important way three-, four-, and five-year-olds learn. They are able to imagine themselves in many situations (for example, what it would be like to go to school), and by doing so, gain a preview of what that experience will be like.

*   Learning is participatory. Children learn that God is the Creator by petting a rabbit, feeling the warmth of the sun, or collecting fallen leaves.

*   Three-, four- and five -year-olds need lots of attention from adults. Group size should be limited to six or eight students.

*   Prayer should be spontaneous (the children pray with their own words) and offered at any time during a lesson.

*   Hands-on activities enhance the lesson; three- and four-year-olds learn better by doing than by being told. They also like to imitate and pretend.

*   Keep activities brief; these children have short attention spans.

Grades 1 to 3 Characteristics

For students in the lower elementary grades, the world is **concrete**—understood through what they can touch and see. The world they are familiar with is regarded as their own **personal** world. These young people are self-centered by nature. They have a short attention span and are easily dis-

▲ *Older adults are an extremely valuable resource to faith communities. Don't overlook their gifts.*

tracted. Children of this age think concretely and learn with all of their senses. They have physical limitations such as the inability to sit still for long periods of time. At this age, the frequently asked question is **"Why?"**

Listed are teaching suggestions to use with students in grades 1, 2, and 3. How might these suggestions be applied to specific lessons or activities?

- Because these students learn best through their senses and not through abstract ideas, use very tangible examples.

- The family is very important to these youngsters; use it as an example to present ideas such as belonging, God's care for us, and community.

- Give each student a turn to participate in class, but help the children to learn how to wait their turn, too.

- The children have short attention spans, so change methods frequently.

- Stories are usually well-received.

- Use physical activities to reinforce your major points, especially if your class period is rather lengthy.

- Stress that each of your students is special—God has created only one of each of them and no one else can be exactly like them. Foster a sense of belonging by frequently calling each student by name.

- To foster a sense of security, establish predictable routines.

- Encourage self-assurance by including some activities the students can accomplish independently.

Grades 4 to 6 Characteristics

Students in the upper elementary grades are beginning to understand the ideas of teamwork and cooperation. They have a growing sense of justice and fair play. Their mental powers are developing and their attention span is increasing. Loyalty can be a strong factor for them. Their sense of responsibility is also awakening. They enjoy collecting things and building models and other such hobbies. This group's most frequently asked question is **"How?"**

Listed are teaching suggestions to use with students in grades 4, 5, and 6. How might these suggestions be applied through specific lessons or activities?

- Offer opportunities for group work; creative projects that utilize the arts, music, and drama can often be quite effective.

- While their faith remains simple, it is no longer naive. They are becoming interested in gathering facts about Jesus and the Church.

- Use methods that challenge their growing memory powers and developing ability to compare and contrast. Such methods engage their interest and elicit their participation. Develop activities or particular parts of your lesson in detail.

- Tell stories, especially those that inform about our history and tradition. The Bible can be read as a "story book." Old Testament stories can be quite effective in communicating their spiritual roots.

- Involve students in short service projects.

- Expose the students to the cultural and historical background of their faith; explain our many religious customs and traditions.

The Church Teaches

Referring to the "Declaration of Religious Freedom," #10–11 from the Second Vatican Council, the *Catechism of the Catholic Church, # 160* teaches that to be human our "response to God in faith must be voluntary; no one should be forced to embrace the faith unwillingly, for the act of faith is voluntary by its very nature."

Recognizing that "God calls people to serve him in spirit and in truth, they are joined to him by conscience, not by external coercion . . . as Christ Jesus clearly revealed," we are told that Christ invited but never forced his hearers to faith and conversion. "He bore witness to the truth, but would not allow force to be used on those who opposed it. For his kingdom . . . is established by the love by which Christ lifted up on the cross draws all people to himself."

A Childhood Lost?

Dorothy Cohen, in *The Learning Child,* observes four noticeable changes that occur in middle-grade children. These are: (1) a loss of spontaneity and the ability to play, (2) a loss of patience, (3) a tendency to be more passive than active, and (4) an increasing cynicism. She points out that the world of the child as it has been known in the past will be lost unless steps are taken by parents and teachers alike to counteract these changes. How would you correct these changes?

Grades 7 to 9 Characteristics

These young people are growing rapidly; consequently, they often feel awkward. They can have frequent and wide mood changes. Their self-concept is developing. Their attention span continues to increase. They have a great deal of energy. This is an age of hero worship; these students may blindly follow fads and peer codes of conduct. They are becoming more independent of their families, especially in relation to peer-group values. They are experiencing a new level of sexual awareness. They tend to deal with moral issues in black and white terms. Morality tends to be formed from external rather than internal authority.

Listed are teaching suggestions to use with students in grades 7, 8, and 9. How might these suggestions be applied through specific lessons or activities?

- Be sensitive and understanding to the diversity in the growth and development of these students. Relate to them as unique persons in a positive manner.

- Present the example and witness of saints and other Christian models.

- Be prepared to channel their energy in creative and constructive ways.

- Continue the presentation of the cultural and historical background of our many religious customs.

- Address the gray areas of life and morality even though the students may find it frustrating to deal with the ambiguities.

- Engage students in activities where they can work together.

- Use their culture: integrate their music, films, television favorites, and sports heroes into your lessons.

Grades 10 to 12 Characteristics

During these years, friendships grow and are appreciated more deeply. Students also begin to be in touch with their inner self. They begin to view themselves as part of a larger, worldwide community of brothers and sisters. Also, dating and relationships between teenage boys and girls take on new significance. They will experience what it is like to be "in love," even if that feeling is fleeting. Sometimes students exhibit a complacency or boredom for practicing religion. They have a strong desire for personal freedom and self-expression, which they exercise with great enthusiasm and a sense of adventure.

Listed are teaching suggestions to use with students in grades 10, 11, and 12. How might these suggestions be applied through specific lessons or activities?

- Be a good listener to any seeds of rebellion, doubt, or boredom that your teenage students have.

- Approach your role as catechist confidently and allow your students to lean on you even if they do not always agree with you.

- Remind them that, as their capacity for independent action grows, they are increasingly more accountable and responsible for their actions.

- Challenge them to pattern their lives after Jesus and his teachings as the Church presents them.

- Involve the students as fully as possible in the life of the parish.

- Be aware of the students' culture and use their culture to make religion practical.
- Deal with moral issues using real life stories.
- Approach religious topics from a personal and relational perspective.

Adult Characteristics

Adults usually have made or are in the process of making important life decisions. Their accumulated experience is their source for reflection. The credibility of outside authority is measured against their life experiences. Adults desire to see immediate results or practical value from the time they spend on an activity. Adulthood can be a significant opportunity for personal development. They want to be able to apply their learning immediately.

How might the suggestions below be applied through specific lessons or activities?

- Involve adults in designing their own continuing religious education process.
- Evaluate frequently to see if the program is meeting participant needs.
- Offer solid, informed leadership as you help adults grow in their faith, but always respect the wisdom they have gained from their own life experiences.
- Include in adult programs some outcomes that participants can use immediately.

Notes

_____

_____

_____

_____

_____

_____

_____

_____

_____

_____

_____

_____

_____

▲ *By early adolescence, students are ready to give back to the community. Plan activities to involve them fully in parish life.*

$\mathcal{P}$art IV $\mathcal{R}$esponse

Making Adjustments

In the opening story, you toured a typical parish's religious education program. You witnessed age-appropriate, vibrant lessons and activities. Now, imagine touring a second religious education program. Drawing upon your knowledge of the developmental characteristics of students at each age level, how would you make corrections (if any) to each catechetical format listed below? Read each of these case studies and then write your comments on the lines that follow. Was the teacher's approach a helpful one? Why? There is no one best answer to any of these situations. Share your recommendations with other catechists.

The Play

The Christmas pageant was the highlight of the school year. Angela, playing the part of Mary, developed stage fright. She told her teacher that she was no longer interested in the part. The teacher said, "It seems to me that you are not happy with something about your role. What can we do to fix the problem?" Angela actually wanted the role but didn't think her hair was appropriate. She and the teacher agreed that Angela could wear a scarf as part of her costume.

_____
_____
_____
_____
_____
_____
_____

▲ _Adults like to see immediate applications for what they have learned._

The God in Us

Dorothy A. Dixon, in her book _The Formative Years,_ writes:

"Spiritual development is not completed in the wondrous beholding of nature, it is only begun. Next there is the development of faith through personal relatedness with other people. Small children think, act, and feel all at the same time. Their relatedness to God is both nurtured and expressed in their relatedness to persons. A child "acts out" his faith in his affection to persons—in a hug, a kiss, and in quiet time just sitting in a larger person's lap. We cherish each time that the child can touch or be touched by persons who care. Indeed, it seems impossible for faith to grow in an atmosphere devoid of human relatedness."

Having a Baby

Mitchell: (age 6) Teacher, you had a baby, didn't you?
Teacher: How nice of you to remember.
Mitchell: I've seen your husband.
Teacher: You're very observant.
Mitchell: My sister's having a baby, but she's not married.
Teacher: Is she now?
Mitchell: Is it okay to have a baby if you're not married?
Teacher: Why do you ask?
Mitchell: I'm happy, but my mother and father are angry.
Teacher: You are looking forward to seeing the baby?
Mitchell: Yes, but it would be nicer if everyone was happy.
Teacher: You want everyone to feel as you feel?
Mitchell: Uh-huh.

Mitchell smiled at the teacher and then gave her a big hug.

Instilling Pride

Peter, 12, had volunteered to work at the parish festival. After he had volunteered, his friend Steve called and offered him tickets to the concert. Because he had given his promise, Peter went to the festival and not the concert, but he wasn't very happy. At the festival Ms. Noel, his teacher, wanted to know why he was so sad. When informed about his decision, Ms. Noel responded, "That was a brave choice you made. You've shown a lot of discipline and character for a person your age. I know that I can trust you because you have integrity and keep your promises." Peter lit up like a Christmas tree. He felt good about himself and was ready to work even harder.

▲ *How are teachers called to adjust to the needs of their students?*

Prayer Response

This section will help you to thank God for the process of your own personality development and growth in faith. (15 minutes for reflection and sharing.)

- Reflect on the path you have traveled in your own personality development. Think of how God has been with you during your journey.

- Read the following Scripture passage, then pause to think how it applies to your life. When you finish, pray the final prayer.

> *"My brothers and sisters, remember that you have been called to live in freedom—but not a freedom that gives free rein to the flesh. Out of love, place yourselves at one another's service. The whole law has found its fulfillment in this one saying: "You shall love your neighbor as yourself"* (Galatians 5:13-14).

Lord, you knew me and loved me even before I was born. Help me to be accepting and loving of myself. Enable me to have a growing understanding and sensitivity toward my students.

BIBLIOGRAPHY

Coles, Robert. *The Spiritual Life of Children.* Boston: Houghton Mifflin, 1990.

National Conference of Catholic Bishops. Chapter VIII, *Sharing the Light of Faith.* Washington, DC: USCC Publications, 1979.

DeGidio, Sandra, O.S.M. "Helping Our Children Grow In Faith," *Catholic Update.* Cincinnati: St. Anthony Messenger Press, September, 1982.

Dixon, Dorothy. *The Formative Years.* West Mystic, CT: Twenty-Third Publications, 1977.

"Effective Adolescent Religious Education," segment one, *Personal Development and Growth in Faith.* Mahwah, NJ: Paulist Press. Video.

Everybody Rides the Carousel. Santa Monica, CA: Pyramid Films. Video.

Harris, Maria. *The Faith of Parents.* Mahwah, NJ: Paulist Press, 1991.

Handbook of Children's Religious Education. Birmingham, AL: Religious Education Press, 1992.

Ministries Growing Together for High School Religious Education. Winona, MN: St. Mary's Press, 1992.

O'Malley, William J. *Becoming a Catechist: Ways to Outfox Teenage Skepticism.* Mahwah, NJ: Paulist Press, 1993.

Sweeney, Richard J. "How God Invites Us To Grow: Six Stages of Faith Development," *Catholic Update.* Cincinnati: St. Anthony Messenger Press, October, 1987.

"Understanding Teenagers," Allen, TX: Tabor. Video.

Westerhoff, John. "Will Our Children Have Faith?" Allen, TX: Tabor. Three 30-minute segments on video.

Nihil Obstat
The Reverend Robert D. Lunsford, M.A.

Imprimatur
The Most Reverend Kenneth J. Povish, D.D.
Bishop of Lansing
June 24, 1993

The *Nihil Obstat* and *Imprimatur* are official declarations that a book or pamphlet is free of doctrinal or moral error. No implication is contained therein that those who have granted the *Nihil Obstat* and *Imprimatur* agree with the contents, opinions, or statements expressed.

Scripture passages are taken from *The New American Bible with Revised New Testament,* copyright © 1988 by the Confraternity of Christian Doctrine, Washington, D.C. All rights reserved.

Copyright © 1994 by the Glencoe Division of Macmillan/McGraw-Hill School Publishing Company. All rights reserved. Except as permitted under the United States Copyright Act, no part of this publication may be reproduced or distributed in any form or by any means, or stored in a database or retrieval system, without the prior written permission of the publisher.

This chapter may be ordered separately using the following ISBN number.

Send all inquiries to:
BENZIGER PUBLISHING COMPANY
15319 Chatsworth Street
P.O. Box 9609
Mission Hills, California 91346-9609

Second Edition

ISBN 0-02-651197-5

Printed in the United States of America.

1 2 3 4 5 6 7 8 9 BAW 97 96 95 94 93

Connecting Learning and Teaching

I hear and I forget.

I see and I remember.

I do and I understand.

Chinese Proverb

In this chapter you will:

- Develop a definition of what it means to learn.
- Describe cognitive, affective, and behavioral aspects of the learning process.
- Explain why each aspect of learning is incomplete by itself.
- Analyze how learning builds Christian character.
- Briefly explain learning outcomes.

Second Edition

Copyright © Glencoe, Macmillan/McGraw-Hill

▲ While children often model their parents' behavior, they also learn from many other sources.

At the Campsite

It was as if all of life's important lessons—those that my family had learned and those that I hadn't—all converged one summer night while camping on the shores of the Saint Lawrence River, about 30 miles from Montreal. As the mother of three children (ages 13, 9, and 4), and an experienced classroom catechist, I had always thought of myself as their primary teacher. I had a lot to learn.

The night began simply enough with a hot dog roast at our campsite on the cliff, high above the river. My husband, Mike, was to join us the next day. As darkness fell, I specifically told myself to walk to the shower before the campground became too dark. Foolishly, I didn't listen.

Coming back from the showers in the near total darkness, I fell down the 150-foot embankment. The tumble seemed to last minutes (it was only a matter of seconds), and fortunately my youngest, Jenny, witnessed what happened.

I found out much later that Jenny was off like a shot. First alerting my other two children, Robbie and Timmy, Jenny went inside our truck and dialed 911 on the cellular phone.

This was fortunate and surprising. Of all the stories and lessons I had shared with Jenny, "what to do in an emergency" was never one of them. I hadn't wanted to "scare" her. Later, my mother asked Jenny where she had learned to dial 911. "On my preschool field trip to the fire station," she said.

Meanwhile, I remained immobile near the bank of the river. Robbie reached me first. I remember just wanting Robbie to pick me up and hold me. Robbie said, "Hang in there, Mom, the paramedics are on their way." When other campers came near, I thought, "Surely one of these people will pick me up and take me out of here," but Robbie wouldn't let them touch me.

My son, an avid football fan, knew what he was doing. He had seen players go down with potentially serious injuries and never were they moved until a doctor arrived. Much later, in the hospital, Robbie told me about a player who had been saved from paralysis because of how he had initially been treated while on the field.

I was airlifted to the hospital with three broken ribs, a punctured lung, and many bumps and bruises. I was rescued in reasonable shape because my family had handled the crisis so well.

In the hospital, I realized that my children had learned in a lot of different ways. I was safe because Jenny had learned on a school field trip, and Robbie had learned from watching football on television. I had to rethink what I thought about learning.

And what of Timmy, my nine year old? The camp ranger who brought him to the hospital told me he had been found hiding in our tent. As I pictured him—alone and frightened—I longed to reach out and hug him. Timmy, I think, could tell what I was feeling. "I'm okay, Mom," he said. "While everyone else was with you by the river, I stayed in the tent and prayed. I thought you might die, but God told me you wouldn't."

My middle child at prayer during the crisis. Where had he learned that? We had prayed together often since he was small, but this was something else. Timmy's prayer was inspired by the Spirit. God had taught him what to do and how to act.

My injuries taught me many other things during the months as I recovered. The most important lesson I learned was that my role with my children is much more than that of a parent or a teacher; I am a learner as well.

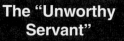

◀ YOUR STORY

In the story, the mother's survival was dependent on lessons that her children had learned in informal educational settings. The variety of ways that they learned points out the vast spectrum of possibilities for education. Write your answers to the following questions.

1. How is television educational? Are its lessons mostly positive or negative?

_____

_____

2. The life-threatening accident turned out to be a learning experience for the mother in the story. How have you learned something valuable from what, at first, seemed to be a negative experience?

_____

_____

3. Timmy proved the success of his mother's lessons on prayer by his actions. If you were teaching prayer in a classroom setting, how would you check to see that your lesson had been understood and applied?

_____

4. Why is it important for a catechist to understand that people learn in a variety of different ways?

_____

▲ *People learn in a variety of different ways. How is this child learning?*

The "Unworthy Servant"

Sofia Cavalletti, in her book, *The Religious Potential of the Child*, expressed the catechist's role as one who cooperates with God in the education of the child. She writes:

The adult who is to proclaim the most essential points of the Christian message, to listen to it with the children, and to observe the children in order to know their needs should remind himself that he is the "unworthy servant" of the Gospel. The adult's function as a mediator is necessary in evangelization; nevertheless it should not be overvalued. The catechist proclaims a Word that is not one's own and assists the child's potentialities, which in no way belong to oneself. The adult cannot help but recognize how often the results surpass the promises of one's work. The adult is so often made aware of the disproportion between what one has given and what the children manifest to possess and to live (p. 52).

Part II Message

What Is Learning?

Notes

_____
_____
_____
_____
_____
_____
_____
_____
_____
_____
_____
_____
_____
_____

There are many popular beliefs about the learning process. Consider the following observations:

- Learning occurs because of rewards and punishments.
- Once something is learned, it is always learned.
- Learning results from "being told."
- Learning is a process of accumulating knowledge.
- Learning transfers automatically.
- Learning should be painful.
- Learning must be pleasant.

Each of the above viewpoints is limited, oversimplifying what actually takes place in the learning process. A balanced learning theory will be broad in its range of activities.

There is no right or wrong way to learn. In the opening story, the mother found out that her children had learned necessary and vital lessons from a number of sources and in a number of different ways. Through their actions, she discovered ways that she, too, could still learn.

Catechist and author Richard Reichert defines learning as:

> *A process of increased intellectual awareness or insight that results in a change in how a person decides, values, or acts. As such, learning is much more than simply coming to know something. Learning is a profound event, a real change in a person's way of living* (A Learning Process for Religious Education, p. 6).

To Reichert, there is a distinction between knowing and learning. For example, a person may **know** that smoking is harmful, but has not **learned** that it is harmful until he or she stops smoking. Learning involves both the awareness and the change.

Generally, people learn in three ways: (1) *Cognitively*—through assimilation of knowledge; (2) *Affectively*—through the forming of one's feelings, attitudes, and beliefs; and (3) *Behaviorally*—through an understanding of one's actions.

Cognitive Learning

People learn through ideas and content. Cognitive learning is the act of incorporating information and ideas into our lives. Cognitive learning has historically seen a major emphasis in general education and in Catholic religious education, with theological content being the subject.

Knowledge of our tradition is important because one cannot understand Catholic tradition without first becoming familiar with the teachings, important persons, and events that shape our faith. Every religious education textbook has content, pointing to the *what* of faith.

Cognitive learning can bring awareness and insight. For example, one might learn about morality through a study of the Beatitudes or learn to pray in a study of prayer.

Affective Learning

Feelings play an important role in the way people learn. Affective learning is especially helpful in religious education when eliciting feelings like contrition, thankfulness, peace, joy, and tranquillity as a part of the lesson objective. Religion is concerned with attitudes and values, not just with reason and logic. Feelings can bring a positive intensity to the learning activity. The enjoyment of what one learns is the spark that ignites continued interest; the desire to learn often has the same effect. And it is no secret that positive feelings of belonging bind people together as a faith community.

Behavioral Learning

Many people learn best by doing. Often, it is in the practice of what we have learned that the knowledge we have gained in the learning process is fully understood. Behavioral learning is especially important to us as Christians. For example, reverence is learned through simple acts, like genuflecting in church or through proclaiming God's Word at the liturgy as a lector. It is what we do, and not just what we say we believe that matters. What we do with our feet and hands (and wallets) are, in some ways, better indicators of our growth in faith than anything we might say. Through acts of justice and mercy and through ritual the Church leads us to knowledge and wisdom.

The Church does more than talk when leading her people. She makes constant use of rituals in which all of us participate. We do not only hear a sermon about Holy Week; we celebrate its reality in tangible ways through ritual.

Pause a Moment . . .

- Reexamine Richard Riechert's answer to the question, "What is learning?" Offer some other examples that show the distinction between knowing and learning.

- List three aspects of the learning process and describe each one in a few words.

- For each of the three aspects of learning, name a personal faith experience that demonstrates that type of learning.

Encouraging Self-Awareness and Responsibility

All catechists would like to see their students acquire the ability to make choices according to Christian virtues, and live them out in daily life. Specifically, catechists hope their students will perceive the meaning of the Gospel message and, in its light, analyze the various choices offered to them and then choose according to Christian teaching. In this way, the students develop the *character* of a Christian.

In many ways, the process of religious education attempts to form this "Christian character" in students. The key to developing character is *self-awareness*. With self-awareness, a person can:

- Demonstrate an understanding of what is taught.

- Distinguish ideas from among several options.

Memo

How do you define learning? How do you learn best?

Erma Bombeck tells the story of a father who laments over the state of his lawn that is under attack from his child's toys. First came the sandbox and then a jungle gym set. Later, when the yard served as the neighborhood campground and basketball court, the father's concern is a cry from the heart: "Why don't I just put the grass seed out in cereal bowls for the birds and save myself the trouble of spreading it around?" His wife's response to all of his complaints was to smile and say, "It'll come back."

Eventually, as children do, the son grew up and moved away. The grass grew perfectly and the lawn became a showpiece. But now the father's concern had also shifted. He asked his wife, "He will come back, won't he?"

- What are the lessons presented in this story?
- How can these lessons be applied to the children you teach?

- Make choices based upon what has been learned.
- Articulate what has been learned.
- Apply what has been learn in various cases.
- Take responsibility for their actions.
- Enjoy, to some degree or other, the learning process.

Through self-awareness, students will be able to know (*cognitive*), feel (*affective*), and repeatedly live (*behavioral*) the Christian message.

The Learning Process and Its Relationship to Teaching

The old saying, "You can lead a horse to water, but you can't make it drink" applies to religious education as well. No one can make anyone learn anything. That's why the art of teaching was developed. What teachers and catechists do is establish an environment conducive to learning in hopes that learning will take place. But whether or not one learns is entirely up to the learner. If we understand how our students learn, we have a better chance at helping them do it.

The teacher and catechist is less the controlling force and more the catalyst who is able to combine knowledge of learning method and student behaviors into meaningful learning experiences. The teacher leads the students into a dialogue with the subject until a new way of thinking is reached. Lessons are applied by the students themselves based on their own circumstances and abilities.

How We Learn

Saint Thomas Aquinas said that all learning occurs after the manner of the learner. That is, learning occurs according to the needs of the learner, not the teacher. It behooves the teacher, therefore, to adapt his or her teaching method to the ways that students learn best. That is why, in order to teach well, it is important that we know something about learning.

Learning takes place through three functions of the brain.

- *Perception* is the ability to receive stimuli from the surrounding environment.
- *Memory* is the ability to recall past experiences.
- *Association* is the ability which allows us to make connections between past experiences and stimuli and relate them to present situations.

Pause a Moment . . .

- What is the role of the teacher in the learning process?
- Why do you think it is important for a teacher to know how learning takes place? Discuss your answers to these questions with a partner.

Some Facts About Learning

James Michael Lee, in his book *The Flow of Religious Instruction*, lists seven findings about the learning process. Consider these findings in relationship to the students whom you teach:

1. Early **family life and background** constitute the most important and powerful variable that affects a person's capacity to learn.

   - How does the family affect your students ability to learn?

   _____

   _____

2. The **environment** in which a person develops, matures, and interacts is a very important factor influencing learning.

   - How do environmental factors affect the students whom you teach?

   _____

   _____

3. People learn best through **direct** experience. Learning always takes on a greater significance when you are the one with the need and desire to demonstrate what you have learned.

   - Offer an example of how you have learned best through direct experience.

   _____

   _____

4. The **meaningfulness** of the learning task is directly proportional to the attainment of a learning outcome.

- Explain who would be more interested in learning a new skill: the single parent who needs a job or the student taking a required course?

   _____

   _____

5. The kind of **reinforcement** given to a particular experience is a powerful determiner as to whether the experience will be learned or forgotten.

   - Recall a lesson that you learned as a child. How was this lesson reinforced by family members, other adults, or peers? How important was this reinforcement in terms of your retention?

   _____

   _____

6. An individual's **need to achieve** is an important factor in learning.

   - Do you find an individual's need to achieve to be primarily intrinsic or based more on the expectations placed on him or her by others?

   _____

   _____

7. **Feelings** are a powerful variable both in the content and the process of learning.

   - What are some feelings the students you teach might have for your subject matter? How can you build your lessons to connect with those feelings?

   _____

   _____

Jesus' Example

"He rose from supper and took off his outer garments . . . He took a towel and tied it around His waist . . . He poured water into a basin and began to wash the disciples' feet and dry them with a towel around his waist" (John 13:4–5).

Was it the lesson taught or Jesus' "hands-on" method that resulted in the success of Jesus' teaching when He washed the disciples feet?

When the teacher is sensitive to the experiences of the learners, the message is much more likely to register with them and take hold. Pope Paul VI said: "Contemporary man listens more willingly to witnesses than to teachers or, if he listens to teachers, it is because they are witnesses" (*Evangelization in the Modern World*).

The New Commandment

"If I, the master and teacher, have washed your feet, you ought to wash one another's feet" (John 13:14).

Part III Discovery

Utilizing the Three Aspects of Learning

The Church Teaches

According to the *Catechism of the Catholic Church,* in order to accomplish social change, it is necessary to appeal to the spiritual and moral capacities of the human person and to the permanent need for inner conversion in everyone. Conversion of heart challenges us to seek cleansing from sin and to conform to the norms of justice, and to further the good instead of obstructing it.

At times, doing something really well is reason enough for doing only one thing. An excellent typist is vital to the smooth functioning of a complex organization. A good painter is an important asset to an auto body shop, a violinist to an orchestra.

Unfortunately, in the case of religious education, doing only one thing really well may not suffice. You may be an excellent motivator of students, while another catechist may be skillful in presenting the doctrine of faith. Someone else always seems better at having students act on the message of the lesson. Any one of us alone is incomplete.

The **cognitive aspect of learning,** by itself, will guarantee nothing. People have to deal with how they feel *(affective)* about what they know. Young adults struggle to do this as they gradually assume responsibility for their own faith lives. Some adults, too, developed questions about beliefs they had taken for granted for years. People also have the responsibility to live *(behavioral)* what they know and believe. By definition, *faith is to be lived, not merely understood.*

Similarly, the **affective aspect of learning** will guarantee nothing by itself. Without an intellectual foundation for support, feelings alone cannot sustain Christian behavior. As long as a person feels good about living Christian values, he or she may not encounter difficulty. But when feelings of satisfaction or affirmation are replaced by feelings of boredom, frustration, or alienation, one's motivation often ceases.

Having positive feelings about something does not necessarily mean a person has grasped cognitively its significance. For example, a memorable experience of belonging *(affective)* to a faith community does not have a lasting effect unless one understands *(cognitive)* what that community is and what it believes. Nor will the experience have a lasting effect unless the person actually participates *(behavioral)* in that faith community.

The **behavioral aspect of learning** also guarantees nothing by itself. People do not normally continue to perform actions when they do not understand the meaning *(cognitive)* or see the value of such actions. One of the reasons for premarital and extramarital sex among Catholic teens and adults is because they lack a coherent understanding of human sexuality. Most Catholics know of the Church's consistent teaching about sexual activity outside of marriage *(behavioral),* but many have failed to grasp *(cognitive)* a clear understanding of the value of living the way the Church has counseled. And, as mentioned above, if one does not feel good about something, it will be more difficult to continue doing it.

Another example of this point is the person who memorizes prayers without having an experience of prayer *(affective)* or an understanding of what the prayers mean *(cognitive).* Such behavior can become meaningless. Young people will find it difficult to act reverently in church unless they first understand the reason for being reverent *(cognitive).*

A distinction made by Richard Reichert summarizes the interplay among these aspects of learning:

> "To know is to have intellectual awareness of datum. To learn is to integrate that datum into a behavior pattern, to use the datum to influence and to shape decisions and actions" (A Learning Process for Religious Education, p. 6.)

Pause a Moment . . .

- Recall a time when your feelings did not support your beliefs. What was the outcome of this difference?

- Which of the following have had the most influence on your moral and religious practice? Habit (repeated practice), beliefs, or feelings?

Connecting Learning with Teaching

▲ *Involve your students in projects, then use the project as a point for learning.*

Just as all learning takes place according to the ability of the learner and not the teacher, so too must the results of the learning be judged by some change in the behavior of the learner. For the catechist, this means that it is necessary to have a clear picture of what the intended learning would look like in his or her student's behavior or performance.

These **learning outcomes** need to be stated at the beginning of the lesson in each of the three domains: cognitive, affective, and behavioral. Learning outcomes are stated in terms of what the students will know, feel, and do to demonstrate that they have learned a concept. It is not enough for the catechist to simply list what he or she will cover in a lesson. This is self-defeating. No catechists teach for their own sake. All catechists intend to make a difference in the lives of their students. The only way to determine whether or not there has been effective teaching is if learning has taken place. Learning can only be determined by the observation of learning outcomes established by the catechist. Robert Mager writes that a learning objective should be the predetermined measure of success:

> "specific enough to clearly state what the learner is expected to be able to do and how you will know when he or she is able to do it. The way the objective does this is by mentioning a performance that will be expected by the learner" (Measuring Instructional Intent, p. 19).

Pause a Moment . . .

- Look at one of your recent lesson plans. Label it with the type of learning it is promoting: cognitive, affective, or behavioral. If you are with a group, summarize and share your list with it.

- Based on your analysis, in what area of learning is your plan the strongest? What area needs the most development? What can you do to strengthen this area?

Naming Learning Objectives

While the overall lesson objectives for the age level you teach are usually established by the program director, the catechist needs to have learning objectives clearly stated in terms of student performance and behavior for each class. Learning objectives state the catechist's intent for the students.

Many times, lesson objectives are written in terms of what the catechist intends to accomplish, not in terms of the intended learning outcomes for the students. If you don't know what to expect from your students after a lesson, how will you know whether they have learned what you have taught?

Here is how these two differ.

- **Catechist Objectives** are written in terms of what the catechist hopes to cover in the lesson. An example: "We will explore the development of the sacraments of initiation in the early Church."

- **Student Objectives** are written in terms of the learning outcomes the students will be able to demonstrate at the conclusion of the lesson. An example: "The students *will be able to* trace the development of the sacraments in the early Church *by citing* three examples of practice from the Acts of the Apostles."

Robert Mager explains that a confusion common in stated learning objectives is the failure to distinguish between *performance* and *abstraction*. Performance is any act you want someone to do. Abstraction is a state or condition in which you might want someone to be. In religious education especially, learning objectives are often written in terms of abstractions. Catechists and directors speak of "building community, increasing one's faith, and becoming a people of prayer." These abstractions must be translated into clearly stated student performances or outcomes; for example: "The student will learn the importance of the community of faith by participating in the family reconciliation service on February 11."

Abstraction Versus Performance

Dr. Tom Walters notes the difference between catechetical objectives for sixth graders stated in terms of abstractions versus those stated as performances. He wonders, "Will everyone agree to these performance objectives?" What do you think?

Abstraction	*Performance*
• Appreciation of liturgical music.	• Sing Gregorian chant daily in the shower.
• Concern for the poor.	• Do two hours of volunteer work each week at the city's soup kitchen. Donate allowance for a month to a hospice.
• A strong prayer life.	• Memorize the Morning Offering. Set aside ten minutes each day for meditation.

Practice writing performance objectives on the lines below, using the following model, "At the end of _____, students will be able to

_____

_____ ."

- Write and share one abstract learning objective.
- Write and share one learning objective in terms of student performance.
- How do performance objectives and learning outcomes presently shape your lessons?

Learning Outcomes in Each Domain

Learning outcomes can be stated for the cognitive, affective, and behavioral domains. Benjamin Bloom, in his "Taxonomy of Educational Objectives" lists various levels of learning under each domain, with each level increasing in complexity. Learning outcomes may be determined by the teacher for each of the levels. For example, in the **cognitive domain,** Bloom's major levels are the following:

- **Knowledge:** the remembering of previously learned material. Learning outcomes include having the student define, describe, or identify common terms.
- **Comprehension:** the ability to grasp the meaning of material. Students will explain, summarize, or give examples to show understanding.
- **Application:** the ability to use learned material in new and concrete situations. Students can compute, demonstrate, predicted, or solve.
- **Analysis:** the ability to break down material into its component parts. Students show an understanding of both the content and the structural form of the material.
- **Synthesis:** the ability to put parts together to form a new whole. The learning outcomes in this level stress creative behaviors and may be described by terms such as devises, plans, revises, or writes.
- **Evaluation:** the ability to judge (based on definite criteria) the values of material for a given purpose. This is the highest of the cognitive levels because it contains all the elements of the other levels. Students show the ability to appraise, discriminate, justify, interpret, or summarize.

For the affective domain, the levels are **receiving, responding, valuing, organization,** and **characterization by a value complex.** Again, learning outcomes are stated in terms of intended student behavior and increase in complexity from level to level.

Mager likes to state the old adage from *Alice In Wonderland:* "If you're not sure where you are going, you're liable to end up someplace else." Or as the Talmud says, "Any road is the right one if you don't know where you are going." For students to achieve the desired learning outcomes demands that teachers clearly understand what the outcomes of the learning will look like at each stage of the lesson process. It means that written lesson objectives will be written in terms of observable student behavior demonstrated at the conclusion of the lesson.

Pause a Moment . . .

- Name one or more learning outcomes you would like to achieve during the next few weeks. How would these outcomes change if they were written for a whole year?
- Name a learning outcome you desire from your class for the coming week in each of these areas: cognitive, affective, and behavioral.

Notes

$\mathcal{N}$otes

Establishing Priorities

Lesson Objectives? Teaching outcomes? By this time you might feel that you are part of the old Abbott and Costello comedy routine, "Who's on First." It's easy to become confused by technical educational and catechetical language. It makes no difference whether you call them learning outcomes or "bigaruts." What is important is that you can identify what it is you hope to accomplish. Once you know that, you can decide on an effective method.

The rest of this section will offer you an opportunity to practice determining and writing clear student-centered outcomes. As you become skilled at identifying these outcomes, you will notice a definite improvement in the quality of your lessons and in the response of your students.

Above all, don't get so caught up in setting objectives that you lose contact with the ultimate reality of why you are a catechist. As the noted catechist Irene Murphy says,

> We sometimes spend so much time planning teachable moments we forget the importance of the sacred. The sacred cannot be defined by a lesson plan, a set of objectives or goals. The sacred is God entering into our lives, as Scripture says, in the brief twinkling of an eye when all is changed (1 Corinthians 15:52).

Lesson planning cannot make the sacred present, but it can make your classes more focused on the subject and, thus, make your students more open to letting God enter their lives. Use the following activities to sharpen your skills.

Setting Objectives

Whether you are in a school or parish religious education setting, it is wise to limit the number of learning objectives desired per course. Generally, cognitive tasks are more appropriate for the school setting since nonschool programs usually meet less frequently.

Dr. Thomas P. Walters stresses the need for full parish participation in formulating realistic learning objectives for a parish, nonschool K–12 religious education program. He lists the following suggestions:

1. **Identify performance objectives by grade.** What should students know *(cognitive)*, what attitudes should they have *(affective)*, and how should they act *(behavioral)*? Textbooks and diocesan guidelines should be used to assist in determining grade-level objectives.

2. **Critique the objectives.** Each grade's objectives should be critiqued by the DRE or principal. Consideration should be taken to insure that the objectives are written in performance terms and that they are realistic.

3. **Select three or four objectives for each grade level for the year.** By the end of the course all the students would be able to do each of these three or four behaviors.

In a school setting where there is more time and the chance to conduct continuous, rather than self-contained, lessons, there would be the opportunity to develop and define more than three or four objectives and more cognitive objectives could be utilized. Nevertheless, the objectives in the school setting must also remain realistic and could be written as performance objectives able to be evaluated from observable behavior. The affective and behavioral areas must not be ignored.

A source of constant frustration to every teacher is when students arrive at the next level of instruction without having learned the "basics," or what they need in order to actively participate in the next level of their development. Although reviews will always be necessary, learning outcomes that are age-appropriate and developmental can go a long way to help students learn what they need to know.

In developing your objectives, focus on those that are appropriate for a particular grade level and that are essential if the students are to continue in their ongoing learning process. How will what your students learn now be developed more fully (and not simply repeated) in later classes? That's what's meant by "developmental;" they lead over time to a fuller knowledge.

If students learn what they need to learn in your class, they will have a solid foundation for lifelong Christian living. If you accomplish your learning objectives, you have no reason to be concerned about whether your students know what they need to know to live as Christians. If your learning objectives are appropriate, your students will know what they need to know **at this time.** Later, other teachers—and the learners themselves—will have the responsibility for additional formation and education.

𝒫ause a ℳoment . . .

- How do performance objectives presently shape your lesson planning?

- What tension do you feel to teach your students "everything they need," and not just your lesson objectives?

- Write two performance objectives for a coming class. Evaluate them in terms of age appropriateness and how they prepare the students for future learning.

Performance-Based Learning Objectives

Dr. Walters writes that "the topic of learning objectives makes many religious educators bristle." Why? According to Walters, it stems from the belief that growth in faith cannot and should not be reduced to observable objectives. There is a fear that by setting objectives, students become more objects than people, and that, somehow, we will squeeze the Holy Spirit out of the process.

However, it is only by establishing performance objectives that a catechist can make a behavioral difference in the students' lives, and thus, evaluate and improve their teaching efforts. Writes Walters:

> *"DREs and catechists, whether they are conscious of it or not, expect their classroom interventions to make a specific difference in the participants' lives. The only way to know if the intended difference*

▲ *Outcome: "Students will work for social justice by taking part in a witness activity."*

occurred is to infer it from observable behaviors. If there is no observable difference in the learners or if the observed difference is not the intended one, there is a problem" ("Where Are We Going? A Case for Learning Objectives in Religious Education," PACE 18).

Lesson plans in religious textbooks often begin with objectives written in terms of teacher behaviors. One way for a catechist to begin writing performance-based learning objectives for students is to translate these into student behaviors and to state the learning outcomes. Consider the following examples. Recall the difference between an abstraction and a performance.

Grade 1

Teacher Objective: To give the children a sense of what it means to have New Life.

Student Behavior: The children will be able to cite examples, like a hatching egg and a blooming flower, that are signs of the "New Life" experienced in Jesus.

Grade 3

Teacher Objective: To begin sharpening observation and interpreting skills.

Student Behavior: The students will be able to define and tell the difference between signs that tell us what to do, signs that give information, signs that stand for something else, and signs that tell how we feel.

Grade 6

Teacher Objective: To challenge the students to follow Jesus every day of their lives.

Student Behavior: The students will be able to list and explain a simple decision-making process that includes the Beatitudes.

While there is usually very little disagreement in the parish over the more abstract teaching objectives, intended performance objectives can lead to heated discussions. Nevertheless, Walters concludes, "it is important to state what the learner should know, feel, believe, or be able to do as a result of the program and to specify the performances that will indicate that learning has occurred."

Pause a Moment . . .

- "It is only by establishing behavioral objectives that a catechist can make a behavioral difference in his or her students' lives." What does this statement mean for you?

- Explain the difference between a teacher objective and an intended student behavior.

Scope and Sequence of Learning Outcomes

In Walter's approach, a parish religious education program should limit its learning objectives to three or four per grade, per year. "In time, this process can result in a realistic and effective religious education program. . . . If this process continues through eighth grade, all students will have achieved twenty-seven carefully selected outcomes" ("Where Are We Going?").

Following Walter's suggestion, write two sample cognitive, affective, and behavioral learning outcomes for the grade you teach. How can these outcomes help the students grow into an active adult faith?

Grade _____

Cognitive

Objective 1: _____

Objective 2: _____

Affective

Objective 1: _____

Objective 2: _____

Behavioral

Objective 1: _____

Objective 2: _____

▲ *How can learning outcomes help the students you teach grow into an active adult faith?*

◁ WRITING YOUR OWN PERFORMANCE OBJECTIVES

Read the following abstract teacher aims taken from various grade levels. Rewrite each as a student performance objective that you will be able to observe by the students' behavior. Make the performance objectives grade appropriate.

Grade 1

Teacher Objective: To encourage the students to make some commitments about supporting one another.

Student Behavior:

_____

Grade 3

Teacher Objective: To help the students share in the joyful message of God's kingdom.

Student Behavior:

_____

Grade 5

Teacher Objective: To lead the student to an awareness of the importance of thankfulness as a Christian attitude.

Student Behavior:

_____

Grade 8

Teacher Objective: To appreciate the students' individual talents and gifts.

Student Behavior:

_____

Action Verbs

Here are some action verbs you can use in stating student performance objectives. You may add others to the list.

Accept	Complete	Find	List	Perform
Agree	Contribute	Finish	Locate	Plan
Allow	Cooperate	Forgive	Make	Prove
Analyze	Color	Help	Move	Recite
Answer	Dance	Indicate	Name	Say
Argue	Disagree	Illustrate	Organize	Tell
Choose	Discuss	Join	Outline	Use
Communicate	Draw	Keep	Participate	Write

Prayer Response

In Luke's Gospel, Jesus is often described at prayer. Read these Gospel passages. Reflect on Jesus' prayer and how he translated his prayer into action: Luke 6:12–16; Luke 9:28–36; Luke 11:1–4.

How is prayer a part of your lesson planning, teaching, and interactions with your students? Write how you can translate your prayer into a specific action.

_____

_____

BIBLIOGRAPHY

Barber, Lucie. *The Religious Education of Preschool Children*. Birmingham, AL: Religious Education Press, 1981.

Cavalletti, Sofia. *The Religious Potential of the Child*. Mahwah, NJ: Paulist Press, 1979.

Foley, Rita. "The Way We Learn," *Create!* New York: Sadlier, 1975.

Lee, James Michael. *The Flow of Religious Instruction*. Dayton: Pflaum, 1973. See Chapter Six.

Mager, Robert. *Measuring Instructional Intent*. Belmont, CA: Fearon-Pitman Publishers, Inc., 1973.

National Conference of Catholic Bishops. "Chapter VIII, Catechesis Toward Maturing in Faith," *Sharing the Light of Faith* Washington, DC: USCC Publications, 1979.

"Overview of Catechetics," session two, *The Learner*. Diocese of Wilmington, video.

Reichert, Richard. *A Learning Process for Religious Education*. Dayton: Pflaum, 1975.

Sacred Heart Kids Club. *Be a Dynamic and Effective Religion Teacher*. Don Bosco, 1989.

Walters, Thomas. "Where Are We Going? A Case for Learning Objectives in Religious Education," *PACE 18*. Winona, MN: Saint Mary's Press.

Nihil Obstat
The Reverend Robert D. Lunsford, M. A.

Imprimatur
The Most Reverend Kenneth J. Povish, D. D.
Bishop of Lansing
June 24, 1993

The *Nihil Obstat* and *Imprimatur* are official declarations that a book or pamphlet is free of doctrinal or moral error. No implication is contained therein that those who have granted the *Nihil Obstat* and *Imprimatur* agree with the contents, opinions, or statements expressed.

Scripture passages are taken from *The New American Bible with Revised New Testament,* copyright © 1988 by the Confraternity of Christian Doctrine, Washington, D.C. All rights reserved.

Copyright © 1994 by the Glencoe Division of Macmillan/McGraw-Hill School Publishing Company. All rights reserved. Except as permitted under the United States Copyright Act, no part of this publication may be reproduced or distributed in any form or by any means, or stored in a database or retrieval system, without the prior written permission of the publisher.

This chapter may be ordered separately using the following ISBN number.

Send all inquiries to:
BENZIGER PUBLISHING COMPANY
15319 Chatsworth Street
P.O. Box 9609
Mission Hills, California 91346-9609

Second Edition

ISBN 0-02-651199-1

Printed in the United States of America.

1 2 3 4 5 6 7 8 9   BAW   97 96 95 94 93

A *Process* for *Planning Lessons*

Textbooks are guides for learning,
summary statements of course content,
and ready instruments of review . . .

Modern texts do more than present information.
[They] . . . foster learning and
stimulate—or discourage—interest.

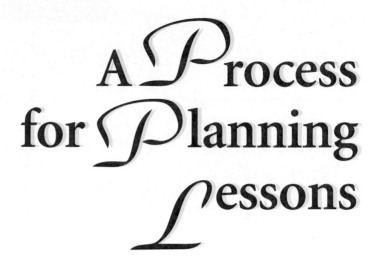

National Catechetical Directory, #264

In this chapter you will:

- Incorporate insights from modern catechetical process into your lesson planning.
- Practice using various features of your textbook.
- Implement basic strategies of long and short range lesson planning.
- Develop a lesson plan that includes the following elements: human experience, message, discovery, and response.

Second Edition   Copyright © Glencoe, Macmillan/McGraw-Hill

The New Commandment

He said to [his] disciples, "Therefore I tell you, do not worry about your life and what you will eat, or about your body and what you will wear. For life is more than food and the body more than clothing. Notice the ravens: they do not sow or reap; they have neither storehouse nor barn, yet God feeds them. How much more important are you than birds! Can any of you by worrying add a moment to your life span? If even the smallest things are beyond your control, why are you anxious about the rest?

. . . Do not be afraid any longer, little flock, for your Father is pleased to give you the kingdom"

(Luke 12:22-32).

Come On, Coach!

Soccer's a simple game; you kick the ball with your feet, hit it with your head, or bounce it off your chest. When on the playing field, you attempt to put the ball past your opponents' goal and keep the ball away from yours. Simple.

But Coach Dan refused to let it be simple. His practices were run like a boot camp. Ten minutes of running, ten minutes of dribbling practice, ten minutes of defense, ten minutes of offense, and a half-hour scrimmage. Players who made mistakes were taken to the side and made to work on the move until they had it right. Dan knew, as if he had eyes in the back of his head, what everyone on the field was doing at all times. And he didn't miss an opportunity to correct them when they fouled up.

The players worked hard and were rewarded for their efforts with improved skills. They won a lot of games, but they had never won the championship. It seemed like every year was a rebuilding year. The core of the team always returned, but the important role players usually chose to play on another team the following year. They liked Coach Dan, but they did not like playing for him. For Dan, soccer had become more than a game; the kids, more than just players. Soccer was the passion of Dan's life and his mission was to make "his girls" the best that they could be. Where the girls played for fun, Dan was driven by a vision of perfection.

His wife, Jean, loved Dan very much and had learned to live with his intensity. He was a kind and generous man who became so wrapped up in coaching that he forgot that the game was for the children's fun and not for his personal goals. She had stopped trying to reach him on this subject a long time ago. He was a good coach, after all.

Their 14-year-old daughter, Sally, was of a different mind. She had played on her father's team for six years. In fact, she had even asked him to coach her at the beginning. Now she was feeling quite differently. She loved her dad, but she didn't want to play for him anymore. She wouldn't hurt his feelings by asking to be on another team or asking him not to coach. So she did the next best thing. She decided not to play this year.

"What do you mean, 'You don't want to play this year?' " Dan asked.

"Dad, I'm ready to try something new. They are forming a drill team at school that I think I'll try out for," Sally answered.

"But what about the team? I can't coach the team if you don't play. What are 'my girls' going to do without me?"

"Your girls! Daddy, we are not 'your girls.' We don't play for you or because of you. We play because we love the game. You've taught us a lot, and we appreciate that. But you haven't taught us to enjoy the game. For you it's all work, all development. Why can't you let us just go out there and have fun?"

Dan was stunned. It had never occurred to him that the young women he coached might not have the same motives and objectives as he had. He could only look at his daughter and stare.

"Oh, Daddy, I didn't mean to say that. I didn't want to hurt your feelings, and now I've gone and done it. Can you forgive me?" Sally cried. She rushed to him and hugged him hard.

Instead of crying, Dan actually laughed. He had learned so much from his daughter in such a short time. Yes, he was hurt, but he also felt relieved. As soon as Sally had said it, Dan knew she was right. He had let his goals and plans get in the way of the players'. He'd have to see what he could do to change the way he coached so that the kids would enjoy playing but still learn what they needed to grow. He hoped his daughter would give him a helping hand.

YOUR STORY

1. What can you identify in Coach Dan's story that applies to your teaching experience?

_____

_____

2. What has happened when you've been narrowly focused on your own lesson plans?

_____

_____

3. What positive things can you draw from the story and apply to your lesson planning process so that the students better grow in faith?

_____

_____

4. How might Sally help Dan improve his approach to coaching?

_____

_____

Notes

_____

_____

_____

_____

_____

_____

_____

_____

_____

_____

_____

_____

_____

▲ *Coach Dan learned that he could not let his personal goals get in the way of his players' needs.*

Four Movements in the Catechetical Process

The Church Teaches

The *Catechism of the Catholic Church*, (#1697) says that catechists have an obligation to be clear about both the joy of Christ's way and the demands it makes. True catechesis will proclaim the newness of life in Christ, informing about the Holy Spirit, grace, sin and forgiveness, the human virtues, the twofold commandment of love, and the Church.

As you know, the goal of the catechetical process is to help people develop a living, conscious, and active faith as stated in the National Catechetical Directory, *Sharing the Light of Faith.* An effective way to do this is by connecting the individual's story with the faith story of the Christian community. This approach has been modeled for you here in *Catechists in Formation* using the terms **Experience, Message, Discovery,** and **Response.**

This approach owes much to the idea of "Christian Praxis" promoted by Dr. Thomas Groome in his important work, *Christian Religious Education,* published in 1980. It is also an approach used widely in catechetical textbooks. The rest of this chapter will explore the steps in the lesson planning process and offer you an opportunity to practice planning lessons in relationship to this process. You will also be given an opportunity to consider other ways of preparing your lesson and setting up a lesson plan book.

Whether you use the four-step approach to teaching the faith, or another, the approach you use will affect how you plan. Suggestions for planning using the four-step method of Experience, Message, Discovery, and Response are offered on the following pages. Note that in each of these steps, various teaching methods are used at appropriate times. Each step requires a different level of planning, and each builds upon the other. These steps work effectively only when they incorporate the various types of learning—cognitive, affective, and behavioral—and when they incorporate worship and music into the process. The students must be treated as active learners, not passive listeners. They must be treated with respect, as people who have something of value to offer to the learning process.

Catechetical lessons that utilize the four-step approach also have as their goal the integration of the Christian Tradition into a lived faith. For the catechist who wishes to help create the right conditions for a student's growth in faith, understanding this process is vital.

Pause a Moment . . .

- What experience have you had with this four-step process? How has your teaching experience been shaped by it?

- How are the lesson in your present textbook developed around these four movements?

The Catechetical Process

A main task of the catechist is to connect religious, scriptural, and doctrinal themes with the life experiences of the students. This is done by breaking down lessons into a series of steps.

Imagine that you have been assigned to teach a lesson about God as the Father. How would you make the connection between human experience and doctrine? How would you get students to respond to that doctrine in a way that made sense to them? Using the catechetical process discussed above, your lesson would follow the steps below. Consider them in relation to the given lesson theme.

Preliminary Step: Lesson Aims

Developing a lesson aim is the first part of every lesson, no matter what method you use. The lesson aim is simply a statement of what you intended the students to learn and how you expect the students to behave—the **outcomes**—from the lesson. What do you hope to accomplish with the lesson? How will you observe this in the students' behavior? Express the aim in concrete terms using one or more sentences. Here's an example:

> **Aim:** *The students will be able to cite and explain one Scripture passage that describes God as Father.*

▲ *To reach your destination, you must first know the path you wish to follow.*

Human Experience

After determining the aim of the lesson, the catechist decides how he or she will help the students name their experience in relationship to the lesson theme (usually given in the textbook). Following a brief sharing session, the students are invited to think about their experience in order to understand its meaning and to remember it. Possible methods include **discussion, guided reflection, role playing,** and **situation games.** For older children you might ask, "How have you experienced acceptance and care in your family?"

At this point, you are framing the lesson. Once the students are in touch with an experience, then move to the next stage. When teaching younger students you will spend more time at this stage setting the scene with simple examples before moving on. The older the students you teach, the more complex examples you can use in this stage. The emphasis here is on **affective learning.**

Message

This step in the process is often considered the core of the lesson development because this is when the catechist presents the community's story, its beliefs, traditions, and practices. Cognitive learning of content doesn't just mean lectures, however. The effective catechist will use various methods such as **story telling, lecture, Scripture reading, drama,** or **audiovisuals.** Here is an example for a seventh grade class.

> *Divide the class into three groups. Assign each group one of the following Scripture readings: Matthew 7:9–11, John 15:1–11, or John 16:25–30. Ask each group to read and share the meaning of the reading and to choose one volunteer to report on the content of the group's passage with the rest of the class. Explain Jesus' use of the term "Abba" and how it helps us know God as a loving parent. Make the connection between the Scripture passages read by the class and Jesus' loving relationship with God.*

Discovery

At this point, go back to the story, exercise, or experience that you used to begin the lesson. You want to tie the students' story together with the Church's message. What difference does the message make in the lives of the students? Effective methods to use here are **questions and answers, personal sharing, imagining,** or **reflection exercises.** Where the prior step is a time to present information, this step leads to understanding. It is at this step that you can measure how well your students have accomplished your lesson **Aim** for them.

Response

It is here that the behavioral aspects of your lesson are most clearly observed. The students are asked to make an honest, free response through prayer or action to the message they have heard. They are asked, "What are you going to do now? Does this message challenge your way of living?" Methods most effective here are **prayer, music** (both singing and listening, recorded or live), **writing, art projects, service, celebration,** or **creating a symbol.** Here's an example:

> *The students will dramatize the disciples' request of Jesus: "Lord, teach us to pray" and Jesus' response. Have a student leader read Luke 11:1–4 to the class. Ask them to imagine that this was the first time they had heard God described as "Father." Have volunteers take the part of the disciples and share their reactions with "Jesus." Conclude the session by praying or singing the Lord's Prayer together. Students are to pray to God as their loving parent every night during the next week.*

Pause a Moment . . .

- What would be some of the other lesson ideas you could utilize in presenting this theme?
- How might you present this same lesson to students in the grade level that you teach?

Advantages in Using This Process

By starting with the students' experience and then moving on to the Church's story, the student will recognize their importance in the ongoing story of the faith. More importantly, they are more likely to remember the Church's message because it has become familiar to them. It also helps the students realize that they are part of a larger faith community.

The community is an important element in all religion lesson planning and in the lessons themselves. The faith story that is shared is the story of the People of Faith. It is a story steeped in tradition and witnessed to by the examples of the millions who came before. It is always through the Church, the believing community, that the catechist's message is proclaimed.

Other benefits of the four-step method include:

- The **aim** sets clear expectations for directors, catechists, parents, and especially students. Students are informed of a behavior that will be expected of them as a result of participating in this lesson. Often, this behavior involves direct contact with the community at large.

- Beginning with **human experience** creates an openness for the message to be received. It helps the students explore the mystery and the questions within their own lives. It helps the students to see that religion is a part, not separate, from what they do and what the faith community does.

- The **message** touches the heart as well as the mind. The performance objectives of the lesson may be cognitive, affective, or behavioral. In the presentation of the message, the students come to see how God has been, and is, present in the experiences of the community of faith—some of the same experiences that the students have already had.

- It is important to have the **discovery** time after the message and the shared experience of the students. If rules, actions, doctrine, and such are presented before the experience, religion may be seen as a set of rules instead of as a way of following God. Bringing the first two steps to understanding together, discovery time allows for personal insight, and time for a healing of the brokenness that may have accompanied past decisions or actions. It is an opportunity to reinterpret experience in light of Catholic teaching. The discovery time also gives room for prayer and the Spirit to do more than a catechist might ever hope to accomplish.

- The time of **response** helps to make the religion class a place where God is, and helps the students to celebrate God's presence. This is the point where students are asked to decide what they will do with what they have learned. Their response to the message translates into participation with the larger community of faith, especially through the Eucharist and the other sacraments. The response also includes service; the main message of the Gospel and the result of how the message affects those who hear it.

Pause a Moment . . .

- In the sharing of human experience, what limits, if any, should you place on the experiences that **you,** as catechist, share with your students?

- What are some ways your students are currently able to participate in Sunday Eucharist and in service projects at your parish? What are some new ways your students might participate in parish life in the future?

▲ *Discovery is an important aspect of learning at any age.*

Part III Discovery

Basic Steps in Preparing a Lesson Plan

Religious education does not happen automatically. Prepared people make it happen. As you plan, keep the following considerations in mind:

Lesson Planning Basics

Effective lesson planning:

1. **Uses three basic tools**—the student textbook, the teacher manual, and you, the person responsible for planning the lesson.
2. **Involves three basic divisions**—the yearly plan, the unit plan, and the lesson plan. Because of these divisions, lesson planning involves long-, mid-, and short-range planning.
3. **Keeps in mind three basic principles**—namely, (1) one hour of teaching requires at least two hours of preparation; (2) lesson plans should always include more teaching material than you will use; and (3) holding the student's interest is directly related to how well you have planned a lesson.

Long-range Planning

As soon as you know the grade level or group you will be teaching, set aside time to get an **overview** of the year. Look through the student text, teacher's manual, and related materials of your program. Review the table of contents which lists the units (major themes) and the lessons (individual topics). Read the introduction to your teacher's manual and become familiar with its style and overall approach to lesson planning. Read through one of the lessons in your teacher's manual. Identify from this the approach you will use and what students will learn during the coming year. These are, of course, your **long-range learning outcomes.**

Practice Mid-range Planning

As the year progresses, generally plan 4–6 weeks in advance of your teaching schedule according to the units or other major divisions of your program. This step will alert you ahead of time to particular materials you may need or any audiovisuals or other resources you will want to request from your program leader.

Approximately two weeks before the class, read the lesson from the student text and underline the main ideas. Carefully read the background information on the lesson included in the teacher's manual, concentrating on the lesson theme. Reflect and pray over the theme and how you will present this particular faith insight in a way your students will understand. Be sensitive to events in your life and those of your students which might relate to the topic. Look for current materials (newspaper or magazine articles, television programs, or current videos) related to your topic. Finalize arrangements for securing any materials you will need.

Notes

The Benefits of a Religion Textbook

Since the days of the early Church, there have been systematic approaches for presenting the basic beliefs and practices of the Christian faith to believers. Communities expressed in writing what they had learned about the Lord so that they could share it faithfully with others.

A religious education textbook series is a valuable resource for any catechist. Professional educators, who have academic and practical experience in the religious education field, plan and prepare these textbooks. Each series tries to present the fundamental teachings, practices, and values of Catholicism. The series, and each textbook in it, is designed for how people learn and their readiness for learning at different age levels.

Textbooks save catechists time. Catechists do not have to create content and place it in sequential order or distribute the content appropriately by grade level. Textbooks provide background information on the material to be presented, supplementary materials for lessons, and a wide collection of techniques for conducting a class session. They are gold mines of information, waiting to be tapped.

However, catechists should consider texts as tools, not ends in themselves. The aim of religious education textbooks is to assist catechists in fostering the students' growth in faith. Through the use of religious education texts and the witness of catechists, the students learn about God and God's revelation; they are helped to experience God and to reflect on their experience. But textbooks can never substitute for the catechist and the students' personal response to God's revelation. Textbooks are resources—something catechists use with students for the students' benefit.

Note that the *Catechism of the Catholic Church* is **not** meant to be a religion textbook. According to a statement published in 1993 by the United States Catholic Conference,

"The Catechism **IS NOT**:
- A text to be used in the classroom.
- A questions and answer book to be memorized.
- A guide to teaching methods and strategies.
- A replacement for current religious education textbooks.
- The exclusive means of catechesis.

The Catechism **IS**:
- An instrument for transmitting the essential and fundamental content of Catholic faith and morals.
- A point of reference for all who have the duty to catechize."

Pause a Moment . . .

- "Prepared people make it happen." Relate a personal experience when you have found out how this statement is true.

- How realistic do you think the long- and mid-range planning suggestions are? How would you modify them to meet your own situation?

Immediate Lesson Planning

Immediate lesson planning usually begins at the conclusion of the preceding lesson. Take a few minutes to make notes about what you want to include in your next lesson. What will you want to review with your students? How will you connect what was learned in this past lesson to the next one? Examine the main points of the next lesson.

During the next few days, allow the ideas a chance to ferment in your mind and in your prayer. For example, if the theme of the lesson is Eucharist, consider what specific aspect of the Eucharist is being stressed. Is the lesson an explanation of why people worship? Is the lesson a study of one of the parts of the Mass? Is it an experience of choosing the intercessions and music for a liturgy? Textbook series usually limit each lesson to one specific topic. Be sure you know what the specific topic is.

About two days before your class, formalize your lesson plan. This task generally takes one hour. You may wish to follow this format:

1. **Prepare a mental inventory of the tools and resources available to you.** First, consider the resources of your textbook series. The teacher's

The first task of lesson planning is to write the objective of the lesson in clear, concise terms. This is usually done by determin-- ing what it is you wish the students to accomplish in a particular lesson. The form of the lesson objective may be as follows:

• "The students will be able to recite the Our Father from memory."
• "The students will be able to look up Scripture references in their Bibles."
• "The students will be able to compare examples of times they have been physically and emotionally healed in the sacraments of Reconciliation and the Anointing of the Sick."

Take some time and practice writing a week's worth of lesson objectives for a part of a particular unit that your class will be studying.

manual contains a wealth of suggestions for a wide variety of prayer experiences, teaching techniques, creative activities, Scripture passages, and media recommendations. Second, outside resources such as current events, contemporary music, television programs, and movies are useful. Third, and most importantly, your own personal experiences and reflections on the main points of the lesson are valuable as you make the connection to the doctrinal message.

2. **Locate the aim of the lesson.** Why is this topic being presented? What result is expected? The answer to those questions is the aim of the lesson. Ask yourself, "At the end of the lesson, what do I want my students to know? to feel? to do?" Your textbook specifies the aim for each lesson. Keeping this aim in mind will lend a unified purpose to your reflections and considerations. At this point, consider the observable student behaviors you will attempt to elicit in order to make sure the lesson aim has been fulfilled. After you have completed your lesson plan, reread it to make sure it accomplishes your aim.

3. **Consider the parts of the lesson.** Each lesson has at least a beginning, a middle, and a conclusion (you may envision four, five, or even more different parts in a lesson). The **human experience** may be considered the beginning, the **message** and **discovery** a part of the middle, and the **response** the conclusion, although you can vary this approach to some degree. For each part, consider the material *(content)* you will cover, how you will cover it *(method),* and the resources you will use. Consider whether the methods and materials of each part will be effective and interesting to your students. Make sure you have enough variety, too.

4. **Determine the time allotment for each part of your lesson.** Take your students' attention span into consideration and make sure the lesson moves frequently enough from one type of activity to another. The time allotment for all the parts should add up to the length of the class period. Plan extra options in case your lesson proceeds more quickly than you thought it would.

5. **Write down your lesson.** Do not fall into the practice of merely checking off parts of the lesson plan in your student text or the teacher's manual. You need to make all of the student text and teacher's manual your own and specify your approach to this particular lesson with your unique group of students. For the most part, lessons prepared only in the head are lessons inadequately prepared.

Set up a lesson planning sheet with these considerations in mind. The following chart offers a possible format for you to use. Divide the work space on the sheet according to the number of parts in your lesson.

Lesson Title: _____ Date:_____
Topic:_____
Aim: _____

Lesson Part	Time Required	Content Covered	Teaching Method	Materials Needed

- Try to analyze your approach to lesson planning. What is one unique, helpful technique you have used?

- Describe your time frame for preparing each lesson. (For example, when do you start to prepare?)

- What time of the day do you plan? Where do you do your planning? Share your experience of the ideal planning session?

- What are some of the other models used for lesson planning? Compare these models to the one listed above.

Follow-up to Lesson Planning

After you have taught the lesson, go back to your lesson plan and jot down your comments about its effectiveness. Did the students accomplish what you had "aimed" for them to accomplish? If you work in a team teaching environment or if you have an assistant, ask him or her to comment on the various parts of the lesson. Such appraisal can easily be added to the first step for planning your next lesson.

Also, if there is more than one catechist on your grade level, you may want to plan your lessons together. By doing so, you multiply the number of techniques for your consideration, thereby enriching each other. Even if there is only one catechist per grade level, sharing occasionally with other catechists can give you new approaches that you had not thought of and opportunities to discuss your classroom experiences.

If you are a new catechist, you will probably find that it takes a great deal of time to plan your first few lessons. This is understandable. You are not yet familiar with the textbook and resources available to you, and you are just beginning to develop your style for preparation. But as the months pass, you will find your own approach to planning and the time required will not be so lengthy.

However, there will never be a lesson that does not require careful preparation. Even the lessons you have taught before will not be the same the second or third time around. The students will be different, with new needs and abilities. You, too, will be different, with additional experiences and insights. Careful and complete planning is an indispensable prerequisite to effective religious education.

- What kinds of learning activities do you favor in your lesson plans? Why?

- How often do you discuss your lesson plan with your program director? with other catechists? Does the director ever review your plans or observe your teaching?

- Do you evaluate your lesson after it's taught? Describe the evaluation process you use.

▲ *Effective teaching requires careful planning which requires a commitment of time, interest, and hard work.*

$\mathcal{P}$art IV $\mathcal{R}$esponse

Planning a Lesson

Take a moment to recall the basic steps of the modern religious education process.

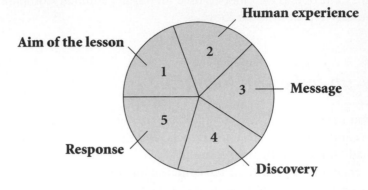

As you plan a lesson, you will need to develop and utilize various activities for each step. You have the opportunity to use many suggested activities for your lessons—many of which are listed right in your teacher's manual—and to develop your own. Remember also that the results of your lesson will be directly related to how thorough a job you did in planning.

The first step of the process—deciding on your aim for the lesson in terms of the intended learning outcomes of the students—is an important one. All of the other discussions, presentations, activities, and evaluations should be structured to help the students accomplish what is stated in the aim.

The aim of a lesson is listed in the teacher's manual. However, most are written in terms of teacher behavior. You will want to understand them in terms of student behavior. Here are three examples:

Teacher Behavior	• To help the students understand the meaning of the Lord's Prayer.	• To encourage the student's participation at Sunday Eucharist.	• To assist the students in witnessing to Gospel values.
Student Behavior	• The students will demonstrate their understanding of the Lord's Prayer by being able to write one sentence explaining each of the verses as listed in the Gospel of Luke.	• The students will sign up and perform one of three services (lector, gift bearer, or greeter) at one of the May Family Liturgies.	• The students will demonstrate Gospel values by serving a meal with parents and catechists at the community homeless shelter on April 10.

The student behaviors do not have to be limited to one or two. They do not have to take place exclusively at the end of the lesson. In fact, appropriate student behaviors should be included in each of the steps of the lesson.

Pause a Moment . . .

- What would be some other ways to express the teacher behaviors listed above in student terms?
- How would you rewrite these two teacher behaviors in student terms? (1) To share with the students God's love for them. (2) To help the students define the meaning of vocation.

Planning Activities

With a specific class in mind, and in light of the process being used, the catechist selects appropriate activities from the teacher's manual or from his or her own personal experience which best fulfills the aims for this lesson. As should be obvious, well written learning objectives make the selection of appropriate learning activities much easier.

Be realistic in your planning. If you know that your meeting place is not equipped with a video recorder and you don't have the time to find a place that is, you should not consider a video as part of your plan. Or, the teacher's manual may suggest a role play for your students to express a certain point. If you already know your students balk at such exercises, why plan it? Try one of the other suggested ideas instead or come up with some on your own.

Here are some questions to ask yourself in planning activities for your lesson:

- Will these activities work for this class?
- How does each activity help teach a particular part of the lesson?
- How do the activities tie in with what is happening in the parish and the students' family life?
- How can I involve the parents?
- What kind of environment do I need for these activities to work?

Another important consideration is how to include the activities into each of the lesson steps. For example, **discussions** and **ice-breaking** type games typically work well in the human experience portion of the lesson, **lecture** and **note-taking** in the message portion, and **prayer** and **reflection** in the discovery. But, again, remember that these are only suggestions. It is possible to use a variety of different kinds of activities in each of the steps.

Pause a Moment . . .

- How realistic are you when you consider activities for your class sessions?
- What kinds of activities (role-play, sharing, journal writing) have you found to be most successful with the students you teach? Why do you think these work for you?

Evaluating the Lesson

When the lesson is over, the catechist should note changes he or she would make in the lesson when teaching it again. Most importantly, the catechist should decide whether the activities fulfilled the objectives for which they were selected. In other words, could the students do what the lesson intended? Did the planned activities help the students to meet the behavior stated in the lesson aim? If not, what would you do differently next time the lesson is used?

Also, remember to save old lesson plans and activity sheets. If you choose to use or adapt them in the future, it's much easier than remaking them from scratch.

Allow others to evaluate the effectiveness of your lesson plans as well. Invite the program director or a fellow catechist to observe your lesson. (This would be separate from a formal evaluation that would be scheduled by the director. This evaluation would take place at your invitation.) Provide your guests with a detailed copy of your lesson plan. Ask them to evaluate your lesson on these criteria:

- The clarity in which you expressed the lesson aim to the students.
- How well you relate to the students.
- How well you presented each part of the lesson.
- Did the activities affect student behavior as you had intended?
- How the lesson aim was ultimately met in terms of student behavior.
- The appropriateness and effectiveness of the methods you used.
- How well you involved each of the students in the lesson.

What would be some other points of evaluation you might want to discuss with the person who observes your lesson plan and lesson?

Effective Activities

Among the many types of activities that may be incorporated into a lesson, role-play, debate, and brain-storming are three that typically work well with students beyond the third grade.

Role-play involves setting up a specific scene for characters (students) to act out. Always allow the students a chance to practice their scene and enough time to be able to perform before others. A follow-up discussion including comments and questions is also necessary. Children of all ages are capable of engaging in role-play, although younger students may need more direction. What is your experience with role-plays?

Debate presents the students with strongly sided issues. Even with younger children, presenting an issue beginning with "Do you agree or disagree with the statement that . . ." is likely to produce a fruitful discussion. Given the age-level of your present students, what might you expect from a debate?

Brainstorming is a form of free association used to generate ideas. There are no right or wrong answers or right or wrong age level. You will want to establish rules for brainstorming sessions, such as: (1) No commenting on anyone else's suggestion; (2) Raise your hand and wait to be called; (3) If your idea is on the board, please don't repeat it; think of a new idea instead. What rules might you add to this list?

▲ *Play can be a very effective activity for catechesis. What lessons could you draw from this activity?*

Here is an example of a lesson used for second graders incorporating the human experience, message, discovery, and response strands. Set up a similar design in your planning book. Use it to plan your own lesson. After you have taught that lesson, refer to this lesson-planning sheet and jot down your reflections on its effectiveness.

LESSON PLAN FOR Grade _Two_ **Chapter** _12_ **Date** _2/15_

Text Title: _Come, Follow Me_

Unit Theme: _Jesus Teaches Forgiveness_

Chapter Theme: _Who Is My Neighbor?_

Pages (S.T.): _pp. 89–96_ **Pages (T.M.):** _pp. 89–96_

✧ ✧ ✧ ✧ ✧ ✧ ✧

LESSON AIM

To introduce the concept of "neighbor" and what this means to our relationships with others.

EXPECTED STUDENT BEHAVIORS

The students will be able to: (1) participate in a discussion about being a neighbor, (2) identify choices which consider others and those that do not, and (3) identify and practice ways of taking others into consideration when making choices.

PROCEDURE

Human Experience Related to the Lesson

Time: _15 minutes_ **Materials:** _2 puppets_

Using puppets to present situations familiar to children, discuss: (1) who are our neighbors, (2) why neighbors are important, and (3) suggestions for broadening the circle of neighbors.

Message

Time: _15 minutes_ **Materials:** _Resource 12A_

(1) Use Resource 12A from Teacher's Support Package. This resource will help students: (1) define "Neighbor," (2) Share Luke 10:25-37 (the Good Samaritan) in appropriate language, (3) Discuss Questions 1-2 on page 94.

Discovery

Time: _20 minutes_ **Materials:** _situation cards_

Pose situations familiar in daily life. Have students offer possible responses. Relate their choices to the Scripture story.

Response

Time: _15 minutes._ **Materials:** _containers and art supplies, paper, pencil_

Make "Helping Containers." Each child decorates can or small container and inserts slips of paper with ideas for loving members of their family or a neighbor as themselves. They are to initiate one idea each day.

Your Evaluation of the Lesson

Small groups need to be assigned beforehand. Allow approximately 10 minutes for the art project. Keep students on track during discussion.

Memo

What are some other questions you might ask yourself when planning activities?

Notes

_____
_____
_____
_____
_____
_____
_____
_____
_____
_____
_____
_____

Prayer Response

Slowly read the following Scripture passage. Reflect on Jesus' words in connection with lesson planning and preparation. Ask Jesus for the patience to thoughtfully and carefully take the time to prepare lessons with the desire of sharing his message with your students.

> *Which of you wishing to construct a tower does not first sit down and calculate the cost to see if there is enough for its completion? Otherwise, after laying the foundation and finding himself unable to work the onlookers should laugh at him and say, "This one began to build but did not have the resources to finish." Or what king marching into battle would not first sit down and decide whether with ten thousand troops he can successfully oppose another king advancing upon him with twenty thousand troops? But if not, while he is still far away, he will send a delegation to ask for peace terms"* Luke 14:27–32.

BIBLIOGRAPHY

Effective Teaching Methods III. 35-minute video. Mahwah, NJ: Paulist Press.

Foley, Rita. "The Lesson Plan." *Create!* New York: Sadlier, 1982.

Hamilton, Betty. "More on Lesson Planning." *Growing as a Catechist.* Edited by Gwen Costello and Carol Clark. West Mystic, CT: Twenty-Third Publications, 1981.

Manternach, Janaan, and Pfeifer, Carl J. "Using Textbooks and Planning Lessons." *Creative Catechist.* West Mystic, CT: Twenty-Third Publications, 1983.

Reichert, Richard. *A Learning Process for Religious Education.* Dayton, OH: Pflaum, 1975.

Religion Teacher's Training Program. West Mystic, CT: Twenty-Third Publications. Video.

Timmerman, Sr. Margaret, MHSH. *How to Be a Very, Very, Very, Very Good Catechist.* West Mystic, CT: Twenty-Third Publications, 1981.

Walters, Thomas P. and Rita Tyson Walters. *Working Smarter, Not Harder: A Survival Guide for Catechists.* Huntington, IN: Our Sunday Visitor, *1991.*

Nihil Obstat
The Reverend Robert D. Lunsford, M. A.

Imprimatur
The Most Reverend Kenneth J. Povish, D. D.
Bishop of Lansing
June 24, 1993

The *Nihil Obstat* and *Imprimatur* are official declarations that a book or pamphlet is free of doctrinal or moral error. No implication is contained therein that those who have granted the *Nihil Obstat* and *Imprimatur* agree with the contents, opinions, or statements expressed.

Scripture passages are taken from *The New American Bible with Revised New Testament,* copyright © 1988 by the Confraternity of Christian Doctrine, Washington, D. C. All rights reserved.
Copyright © 1994 by the Glencoe Division of Macmillan/McGraw-Hill School Publishing Company. All rights reserved. Except as permitted under the United States Copyright Act, no part of this publication may be reproduced or distributed in any form or by any means, or stored in a database or retrieval system, without the prior written permission of the publisher.
This chapter may be ordered separately using the following ISBN number.

Send all inquiries to:
BENZIGER PUBLISHING COMPANY
15319 Chatsworth Street
P.O. Box 9609
Mission Hills, California 91346-9609

Second Edition

ISBN 0-02-651202-5

Printed in the United States of America.

1 2 3 4 5 6 7 8 9 BAW 97 96 95 94 93

Effective Teaching Techniques

❖

The quality of catechists is more important than the quality of their tools. But good tools in the hands of skilled catechists can do much to foster growth in faith. Catechetical "tools" are many and varied. They include human and organizational resources, the communications media, textbooks, and audiovisual materials.

National Catechetical Directory, #249

❖

In this chapter you will:

- Practice creative lesson planning tips.
- Demonstrate effective ways to increase student participation through the use of questions.
- Develop your own unique lesson planning techniques based upon commonly used methods.

Second Edition

Copyright © Glencoe, Macmillan/McGraw-Hill

Evaluation

▲ *An informal way of measuring effectiveness is to look at your students. Do they enjoy being in your class? Are they eager to participate?*

"Dennis, I thought we were going to get pizza tonight?" Hali whined. "We're not going to learn something, are we? You promised." This was the last meeting before summer, after all.

Dennis Kelley turned off the CD player and said, "Everyone come over and have a seat. I have one last assignment for you and then we can go for pizza." The crowd moved to be seated, groaning as one.

Dennis looked at the group—17 ninth and tenth graders—and thought, how had the year gone? He remembered the first meeting. The kids had come with their parents. The pastor and DRE explained this new approach: a catch-up and review course on the Catholic faith for high school students.

When it had been Dennis's turn to speak at that first meeting he asked the parents and kids to stand. Then he instructed the parents to turn around and face the wall. To the high school students he asked, "Was it your own choice to come here tonight? Signal 'yes' by blinking your right eye. Signal 'no' by blinking your left eye." From this exercise, Dennis knew that reaching these teens would be a difficult task since they were here not of their own free wills.

Nine months later, three of the original group had dropped out, but four others had joined. Early on, Dennis got the idea that they liked the format better than he had expected, or at least, they didn't seem to mind being there. Now he would find out for sure. It was time for the final evaluation.

"You need to answer these questions," he said to them. "Please be specific. You don't have to include your name."

Here's the form that Dennis handed out:

Youth Group Survey

1. Describe one change in your faith life from the beginning of the school year to now.

2. Which of the Sunday night meetings did you like the best? The least? Why?

3. What did you like about the Sunday night format? What did you dislike? Why?

4. In what parish activities would you like to participate?

5. Will you be returning next year?

Finished, the group went off for pizza with the parent moderator. Dennis waited behind because he couldn't wait to see what they had written. There were 14 "yes" responses and three "I don't knows" to question 5. That was the litmus test. If they were willing to continue, he must be doing something right. He could now eat pizza with them in peace.

As he walked to the pizza place, Dennis continued to read. What had been their favorite meeting? Dennis was surprised. The majority chose a lesson on the passion and death of Jesus held on Passion Sunday. What could they have liked so much about that?

Dennis replayed the lesson in his mind. They had written their own obituaries as the opening activity. "What would you like to be remembered for?" he had asked. In small groups, they discussed what they knew about Jesus' arrest, sentencing, carrying of the cross, and crucifixion. It was a familiar story. "I liked that night because I already knew what happened," one person wrote.

Dennis had mixed up the completed "obituaries" and passed them out again randomly. When they shared each other's obituaries, the experience had been very moving. They had mentioned what kind of people they hoped to be, not bragged about what they would do. The session ended with a classic video about the passion. "The video made me cry," someone wrote.

What had made the lesson such a success? The variety of the planned activities? The incorporation of prayer? Dennis wouldn't know for sure. The evaluation didn't go into that much detail. He would have to ask them, but not tonight; he had promised not to interfere with their pizza.

SELF-EVALUATION

It's your turn to evaluate your own work. Think back on the lessons you have presented during the past few weeks, then answer the following questions. If you are with a group, share your responses with a partner.

1. Describe one change in your faith from the beginning of the school year to now.

_____

_____

2. What part have your students played in your personal faith journey?

_____

_____

3. Which was the most effective class that you've recently taught? What made it so effective?

_____

_____

4. What kinds of activities were the students engaged in during your most effective lesson?

_____

_____

5. Judging from this experience, what are the key ingredients for an effective lesson?

_____

_____

Notes

The Role of Experience in Religious Education

▲ *"Learning by doing" experiences can make cognitive learning come alive.*

Dennis had wondered during the course of the year if he was reaching the students and if they were responding to his teaching. The survey results revealed that his religious education program was effective.

The *key* to effective religious education is in the approach to the lesson. Although it is important for the catechist to have a proper understanding of the religion and theological doctrine, this understanding alone is not enough. Students need a varied and attractive learning experience in order to remain attentive and interested. Effective religious education is not so much a matter of having the **answers** as it is a matter of having the approaches to the students' real **questions.** In Dennis's lesson on the passion and death of Jesus, a variety of techniques were used to present the key points of the story and to actively engage the students in the learning process. This is one of the reasons the students liked the lesson.

The *goal* of religious education is the students' growth in faith. Properly explaining content will not assure that this goal is reached. Facilitating growth in faith involves teaching what can be practiced. Catechists need to involve the students in the learning experience so that they examine, question, enjoy, understand, choose, and connect the message to their daily lives.

During the 1960s, major innovations were introduced into religious education. The changes generated a long debate over which took priority: *Content* or *method?* One side stressed the importance of the content of religious education, meaning theology or doctrine, while viewing catechetical (educational) method as merely a *delivery system*. The other side stressed how the content or doctrine was presented. However, the purpose of both sides was the same: to promote the students' growth in faith. Lived faith unites both the content and method into practice.

Looking back, the debate seems naive. We now know that using effective teaching methods helps the catechist to clarify the content and maintain the students' interest. We also now know that people do not learn something simply through being told or through memorization, although these are part of the learning process.

Religious education today is based on the principles of *experiential learning*. Most major textbook series begin their lessons by considering an aspect of the students' lives. Then, a doctrinal message is presented. Finally, a connection is made between the two. This view stems from a holistic view of faith that integrates the working of the mind, spirit, and body.

This experiential approach parallels the way humankind has come to recognize God's presence. That presence was made known through major events in the lives of God's people. As the ancient Hebrews reflected upon God's action in their lives, they realized God's concern and love for them. When they considered the meaning of their experience, they began to perceive the content of God's revelation to them. They told their stories and developed their meanings for generations before writing them down.

The experiential approach does not diminish the importance of the Gospel, theology, doctrine, or the Tradition of the Church. Rather, it emphasizes the

The Importance of Experience

Experience is of great importance in [religious education]. Experiential learning, which can be considered a form of inductive methodology, gives rise to concerns and questions, hopes and anxieties, reflections and judgments, which increase one's desire to penetrate more deeply into life's meaning. Experience can also increase the intelligibility of the Christian message, by providing illustrations and examples which shed light on the truths of revelation. At the same time, experience itself should be interpreted in the light of revelation. (*National Catechetical Directory*, #176)

process by which people are able to discover the meanings of these truths, as they appear in the contexts of their own lives, and live out their implications.

Pause a Moment...

- How do you see the traditional understanding of content as doctrine fitting into experiential religious education?

- In what ways have you grown in faith: through hearing or reading content? through personal experience? through prayer?

Choosing the Proper Learning Activities

Memo

Examine a lesson plan from a recent session. Make notes of the changes you could make either in the content or method. Then, examine the lesson from the students' perspective. What changes would you make to the lesson now?

There is no single teaching method or approach that should always be used to the exclusion of other techniques. Many methods are equally effective in presenting the message of faith and facilitating the students' learning experience. And, because certain techniques are more appropriate and effective on some grade levels than on others, a **variety** of teaching techniques is essential. Teaching is a lot more than telling!

Effective catechists are not afraid to experiment with new methods or try new approaches that might work better with their group of students. Once they find something that works, they incorporate these methods into their teaching. Choosing appropriate methods depends on the goals or objectives of the lesson. It starts with asking, "What are the desired outcomes for this lesson?"

When selecting a technique for a lesson, keep in mind that people learn in three ways:

1. **Cognitively**—through acquiring ideas, absorbing facts, and the content of knowledge from a given tradition.

2. **Affectively**—through feelings and attitudes.

3. **Behaviorally**—through actions and experience.

Lessons should include a variety of approaches in order to reflect these three ways of learning.

Methodology and approaches become catechetical when they are used to create conditions that encourage people to seek, accept, and integrate the Christian message more fully into their lives. Religious education goes beyond handing over a body of truths

Some methods are especially effective for religious education. Catechists can weave into lesson plans various experiences of prayer, liturgical participation, Christian service, and opportunities for public witness. Finally, remember that methods are only tools. They merely set the stage for the students' possible growth in faith and never force or guarantee it.

Pause a Moment...

- How can a student's life experience affect a religion education lesson?

- How does the process of revelation in Scripture parallel the process of learning in religious education?

- From which type of learning activity do you usually learn best? enjoy most? grow in faith?

The New Commandment

Jesus taught through stories:

"A man had two sons, and the younger son said to his father,"

(Luke 15:11-32);

Jesus also taught through examples:

"Learn a lesson from the fig tree. When its branch becomes tender and sprouts leaves, you know that summer is near"

(Mark 13:28-31);

and Jesus also taught by doing:

"While they were eating, Jesus took bread, said the blessing, broke it, and giving it to his disciples said, 'Take and eat; this is my body'"

(Matthew 26:26-30).

Can we do the same?

Putting Variety into a Lesson Plan

Before considering specific ways of adding variety to your teaching, it is useful to briefly review the basics of lesson planning. (For a complete discussion of lesson planning, see Chapter 6, "A Process for Planning Lessons.")

1. **Clarify the lesson topic**. Decide which aspect of the topic is being stressed in the lesson. Make sure it is not a vague collection of many topics.

2. **Decide on the aim.** Why are you presenting the topic and what results do you expect? The answer to those questions identifies your aim. Having the aim clearly in mind keeps all reflections and considerations focused on a unified purpose.

3. **Consider the parts of the lesson.** Recall that they are *human experience, message, discovery,* and *response.* For each part, consider what will be covered and how, and what materials are needed. Remember that each lesson has at least a beginning, a middle, and an end.

4. **Determine the time needed.** Consider your students' attention span when you determine the frequency with which you move from one type of activity to another. The time allotment for all the parts should add up to the length of the class period.

Now for the sake of discussion, assume that a lesson begins with a series of questions reviewing last week's material. Next, the initial point of the new lesson could be introduced by asking a series of questions that relate to the students' personal experiences. Then, a discussion could be held on the implications that the topic has for the students' daily lives. These three parts of the lesson may seem different to the catechist. But the students experience this as one lengthy section in which the method is the same—use of questions and answers.

Consider how you could vary the methods in this hypothetical section of a lesson.

- Review last week's lesson by dividing the class into two groups to compete in a game like tic-tac-toe or "Hollywood Squares."

- Introduce the new lesson with a video.

- Through class discussion, consider possible ways the point of the lesson might relate to the lives of the students.

If you were to use a variety of methods, the students could experience frequent movement from one type of activity to another. What happens if we simply rearrange the sequence of the lesson? Instead of the original order (*discussion, discussion,* **project**), rearrange it to *discussion,* **project,** *discussion.*

As a catechist, you are a designer of learning and faith-growth experiences for your students. As you gain experience, you will discover ways in which the composition of your lesson can be varied to achieve more student interest and participation. Try not to be limited by your own experiences of religious education. Attempt variety, try to be creative, and, above all, enjoy what you are doing.

A word on creativity: Select the method to use based on the desired outcomes of the lessons, not on what is most creative. Choose the activities based on which best reach your students, not on what seems the most fun.

If there are a number of catechists in your parish, consider meeting together to share lesson plans and approaches. Some of their ideas may be valuable in your own teaching situation. Devote some of the meeting time to analyze why a particular lesson was successful. Remember, reasons for success or failure are more important to future effectiveness than the successes or failures themselves.

Pause a Moment...

- Describe a lesson that utilizes a variety of methods or teaching approaches.
- Which means of varying your lesson do you find most effective? least effective? Explain.

◄ EXERCISE

Review one of your lesson plans. In the first three columns below, list the content, learning objectives, and teaching methods from the lesson for each movement. In the fourth column, decide how you would teach the lesson with more variety.

Movements of the Catechetical Process	Content	Learning Objectives	Teaching Methods	Variety
Experience				
Message				
Discovery				
Response				

Look over the next lesson you will teach. Think about the unique needs of your particular group of students. Then, design a varied approach to this lesson or part of this lesson.

Learning Objective	Teaching Method
_____	_____
_____	_____
_____	_____

Consider a possible catechist meeting. How could such an opportunity be structured to be of value to you in making your lesson plans more varied and effective?

_____

_____

_____

Varying Your Pace

Pacing or timing a lesson is a valuable skill that improves with experience. Effective teachers pace a lesson to students' rhythms:

- **Speed up** if students are restless.

- **Slow down** for note taking, to give directions, or to continue a prayer time.

- **Change activities** if students are distracted, if the activity is too difficult, or if students are fatigued.

An Overview of Commonly Used Techniques

As you gain experience as a catechist, you will develop your own particular style and learn your own unique techniques. There are many ways to encourage group discussion, individual and group projects, and many ways to utilize audiovisual materials. This section will present basic fundamentals in these areas. The scope of the chapter does not permit a full treatment of teaching techniques. What is presented offers a few of the possible techniques catechists can use.

Structuring Student Discussion

Many catechists know the feeling of having enthusiastically prepared a lesson with a good variety of methods only to have the students stare into space with glazed eyes once the lesson begins. Whatever the cause, the catechist feels the void and learns firsthand that class participation is absolutely crucial. If it is lacking, the lesson becomes a lecture. It becomes very difficult to determine whether the students understand what is being presented.

The first task is to help the students to feel comfortable. Often, in a religious education setting, the students come from many different schools and do not even know each other. Several ice-breaking games that might simply be used for teaching each other's names are often an appropriate opening activity.

▲ *Role plays are very effective teaching methods.*

Notice which students participate in discussions. Watch for the *dominator,* the individual who has the answer to every question. Quite often dominators are very bright, articulate people who have the correct answer to most questions and are not afraid to speak in class. They guarantee a response to the catechist's questions, but the more a dominator participates, the easier it becomes for the rest of the class to lose interest and become passive. Insist that the dominator receive permission (usually by raising a hand) before speaking.

Some students are *reluctant participants*—quiet or timid in most situations. They feel that they risk being wrong or ridiculed when answering a catechist's question. From their perspective, such individuals feel they are most vulnerable to harm at this moment. For these students, hearing the sound of their own voices can be an important break through. These students will participate if encouraged. This can be done by asking a question of the person near him or her, and then asking the reluctant participant, "What do you think of that statement?" When reluctant participants do express an opinion aloud, it is important to affirm their participation.

In order to attain total student participation, use the following strategies:

1. **Prepare your questions.** Very few catechists can ad-lib effectively. A fuzzy question will prompt a fuzzy reaction from the students. Use the teacher's manual for possible suggested questions. Formulate some of your own. Consider your options for reinforcing the content and

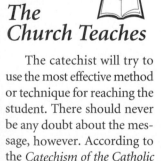

The Church Teaches

The catechist will try to use the most effective method or technique for reaching the student. There should never be any doubt about the message, however. According to the *Catechism of the Catholic Church,* #1698, Jesus Christ, the way, the truth, and the life, is always the point of reference for catechesis.

consider the differences among your students. *Write down* the questions that you will use. Be sure they are concrete and to the point.

2. **Use an opinion question to begin a discussion.** Anyone can answer a question that begins with "What do you think about . . . ?" In opinion questions, there are no correct answers. They differ from fact questions (for example, "What are the names of the 12 apostles?") that do have a correct answer. Which question would you rather be asked? If you were asked to give the names of the 12 apostles, there is a very good chance of being wrong. If you were asked why you thought Jesus chose the 12 men he did to be his apostles, you can participate without fear. Which chance do you prefer to take? Remember, your students have similar feelings. Opinion questions allow students the freedom to participate in your class without the fear of being wrong.

3. **Use variety.** Opinion questions, fact questions, example questions, easy questions, difficult questions should all be included in your mix. The quality and variety of questions used can help or hinder student participation.

4. When there is a choice, **always call on a slower student,** especially before most of the points you are seeking have been mentioned. Give the slower and more timid students the first chance at being right.

▲ *Use a simple rule, "Raise your hand to speak," to encourage reluctant students to participate.*

If various types of questions are used and the reluctant students are selected, those students will become more involved in the lesson and overcome their feelings of shyness. The message sent to your class is that everyone's ideas are important to you, and that no one will be allowed to simply be an observer. Do not avoid the dominators, but use them to answer the more difficult questions. They will always find a way to participate and they add a great deal to the class. Ideally, your goal is to evenly distribute participation opportunities among your students.

Getting the students to participate is not always the problem. Sometimes, students give answers that are completely unrelated to the question. Do not pretend there is a connection, or credibility will be lost with the rest of the class. Without being abrasive, simply say, "No, that is not what I was looking for. Does anyone else think he or she has the answer?"

Sometimes there is no response to the question. In this case:

- Ask the students if they understand the question.

- Restate it in different words.

- Call on one of the brighter students to answer the question.

If the students frequently do not understand your questions, the wording may be too vague. Spending more time preparing the questions (write them out and read them aloud to yourself) can solve this difficulty.

Sometimes several students will answer at once, resulting in confusion. Establish a procedure for calling on students, so that slower students will not be left out. This enables everyone's answers to be heard by the class. Insist on proper behavior during the discussion activity.

Using these strategies and types of questions, along with encouraging students to add their ideas to the discussion, will increase the classes' participation and learning. Use student responses to build to the points you want to make.

Helping/Hindering Communication

The words or phrases that we choose can either help or hinder effective communication.

These phrases encourage communication:

- Tell me about . . .
- Please explain how . . .
- Help me understand . . .
- Did I understand that . . .?
- Let's talk about it . . .
- Are you saying that . . .?
- Do you mean that . . .?

These phrases hinder communication:

- That's not right.
- I don't believe you.
- You are too young to understand.
- I don't think you understand.

Of course, sarcasm, ridicule, and making fun of a student has no place in the classroom, especially from the catechist.

Different Types of Questions

The following types of questions will help you achieve greater student participation. Try to divide the opportunities for participation evenly among the students.

• **Boomerang questions** can be used to turn students' questions into opportunities for class participation. Instead of immediately answering a student's question, reflect it back to the group for their consideration: "That's an interesting question, John. Does anyone have a possible answer?"

• **Comparison questions** develop critical thinking skills: "How would you compare the story of the Good Samaritan to the way the class outcasts at your school are often treated?"

• **Example questions** allows the students to illustrate some point of the lesson: "Can you give me an example of how Jesus helped the sick?" "What is one example of how you could show more kindness to your brothers and sisters?" Example questions provide measurable evidence of what students have learned.

• **Fact questions** reveal what the students remember: "Which book in the New Testament gives a description of life in the early Church?"

• **Opinion questions** are appropriate at the beginning or middle of a discussion: "Why do you think the Samaritan stopped to help the man lying at the side of the road?"

• **Opinion surveys** identify what the class is thinking, and let everyone participate: "One at a time, tell me which commandment you think is most important."

• **Pull-in questions** are simply a way to include other students in a response that has already been received: "Can anyone add to that point? Does anyone feel differently?"

• **Repetition** of questions later in a lesson is a good way to drill for understanding.

• **Review questions** reveal whether your students learned the major points of a previous lesson. They can also be used at the end of a class regarding material that was just presented.

▲ *Add variety to your discussions by using current newspaper or magazine stories.*

Pause a Moment . . .

• Who are the "dominators" and "reluctant participators" in your class? What strategies can you use with each type of student?

• What do you find necessary for good class discussion?

• How many different types of questions described in this section have you used with your students this year?

The Catechist as a Technique

Usually people are not thought of as techniques, but the catechist has a tremendous effect on the overall class situation.

• **Attitude.** The catechist's attitude is contagious to the students; they will "catch" both enthusiasm and indifference. Watch to see how your behavior and attitudes affect your students. Ask yourself, "Do I enjoy what I am doing as a catechist?" If you can't answer "yes," your attitude may have a negative effect on what happens in the classroom.

• **Eye contact.** First of all, eye contact makes each student feel noticed and regarded in a positive way. Second, eye contact helps to maintain student attention and cuts down on discipline problems. Third, it helps to build enthusiasm for the lesson.

• **Movement.** Catechists who move around the room effectively engage the interest of the students. The catechist becomes a moving target for the students' attention. Movement puts the catechist close to each student during the class session, indirectly promoting discipline. Coming out from behind a desk or podium lessens the barrier between the catechist and the students and leads to a more creative classroom atmosphere.

Pause a Moment . . .

- Describe how an effective catechist uses the techniques described above.
- How would moving around the classroom help you to prevent potential student behavior problems?

Using the Board to Enliven Your Lesson

The chalkboard, whiteboard, or large easel pad are teaching tools that often go unused. When using these tools:

- Avoid turning your back to the class for a prolonged period. This lessens eye contact and can interfere with student attention. It also invites discipline problems.

- Write in many different directions, from top to bottom, side to side, in blocks of space, or in circular motions. In this way, the board becomes a dynamic and effective tool that holds their attention.

- Do not be concerned with precision and neatness. It is only necessary that the students understand the ideas presented. Explain each part of the lesson as it is put on the board.

- Underline or circle items you want to stress, twice for added emphasis. Draw a line between items you want to connect. To omit something or deny its importance, simply cross it out. Use asterisks, boxes, or capital letters to emphasize words. Include symbols and simple illustrations. Be spontaneous. There is no one way of using the board. In time, you will develop your own approach.

The chalkboard or whiteboard is an interest holder because it presents a picture that is developing and not complete. Students follow the catechist as various words and illustrations fill up the board. Periodically letting students write on the board is a special treat that actively involves them in the learning process.

Although a valuable tool, the board can be overused. Keep the board an active learning prop, using it to hold students' attention, involve them in the activity, and keep them from boredom.

Using Stick Figures

Drawing stick figures on a chalkboard or whiteboard can be a simple way to illustrate a point in a lesson. It is not necessary to be an artist to use stick figures. Examine the examples to the side to see how different facial expressions can be used to illustrate your point or how hands and feet can tell stories. Different angles bring animation to the figures. Experiment for your own special variation. You may be self-conscious at first, but after a few classes, you will gain confidence in this simple technique.

Pause a Moment . . .

- How often do you use the board as part of your lesson?
- What is your experience of using stick figures?

Basic Figure

Happy

Angry

Holding an Object

Stick Woman

Sitting

Utilizing Creative Projects

Creative projects can be used as part of a lesson and can be developed by following several simple steps:

1. Introduce the project by explaining why it is important and how it relates to the lesson. Then give the students directions to complete the project.

2. Have the students begin the project. While they are working on it, walk around the room. Check to see that everyone understands the directions. Later, double-check their progress. This is an opportunity for indirect, individual teaching. Walk among the students a third time toward the end of the project to encourage them to finish their work.

3. When work time is over, have each student display and explain his or her project to the rest of the class. Instead of a very simple item merely announced by "now we will do our project," this section can become a number of different elements.

Projects

Projects are used because they bring a variety of methods to the learning experience. Projects might include creating class banners, conducting canned goods drives, or preparing a class worship service. Because of their tangible nature, projects leave a deep impression and help the students to retain the message of the lesson.

When using projects:

1. Do a sample of the project ahead of time. What will your students learn from the experience? Is it age appropriate? Can it be done in the time allotted?

2. Make the instructions clear and complete. Repeat the instructions at least once, because someone will not understand them the first time.

3. Collect the necessary supplies in advance. Don't do the project if you don't have what you need to complete it.

4. Be aware of time limitations when selecting a project. Some projects take a long time when done by small, inexperienced hands.

5. Stay with your students as they work. This can be an opportunity to get to know them better and to informally reinforce a point of your lesson.

6. Be sure the project is a learning experience. Refer to it from time to time when reinforcing one of the points of the lesson. If it's busywork, the students will know.

Pause a Moment . . .

• Using a recent lesson as a starting point, brainstorm some possible projects to use at various points of it.

• From your experience, what is the most important thing to remember when planning a project?

Notes

Audiovisuals

Videos and filmstrips are extremely effective means of involving students on the affective level. While they do offer a more interesting way to present the information component of a lesson, they are best at revealing the human experience and evoking a response from your students. They can also be used to develop specific aspects of the lesson or to establish the main idea in a presentation.

Follow these suggestions for using audiovisuals as part of a lesson:

1. Know why you are using the audiovisual and what students will learn from it. The audiovisual should always be an essential part of the lesson, never an add-on or time-filler.

2. Preview the audiovisual and know how you will use it. Do not show something you have not seen or that does not accomplish your aim.

3. Have the media equipment ready and know how to use it. Make sure that everything is in running order.

4. Prepare the students for what they will see. Establish the main idea you want them to learn. Give them one or two questions in advance to answer from the audiovisual to keep them focused on the task.

5. After the viewing, follow through. Discuss the questions you gave and or use a project to see if the students grasped the point. Also explore how the message of the film can be applied in the students' daily lives.

While audiotapes have a limited appeal for direct classroom use, they are very effective for your personal ongoing education. Check with your director for resource catalogues that list such tapes.

Pause a Moment . . .

• Does your parish or diocese have a media library? Where else can you acquire appropriate media for your students?

• Using a recent lesson as a starting point, brainstorm some possible ways that you could use an audiovisual.

Audiovisual Alternatives

No matter how much students may complain about having to work, they much prefer to be an active participant in a project than a passive viewer. For all of their merits, audiovisuals often promote passive viewing or listening. To encourage active participation, do the following:

• Have students develop their own script and put on a short play or skit. You can have them do this from scratch or have them watch an audiovisual, then turn off the projector before the finish and have students dramatize how they think the audiovisual should end.

• Teach students songs, or have them make up their own. Have students write new lyrics to sing along with their favorite songs.

• Encourage students to make up dance steps and hand gestures to express how they feel or to communicate what they have learned.

▲ *Don't be afraid to use your musical talents as part of your lesson.*

▲ *How do you make creative projects part of your lesson planning?*

Part IV Response

Putting It into Practice

The following activities apply the major points covered in Part III of this topic. Complete each activity on your own. You may be asked to share some of your ideas with others.

Review of Teaching Techniques

How can you use the techniques described in Part III most effectively?

Teaching Technique   **Ideas for Effectiveness**

Questions and Discussion Techniques

_____

Person of the Catechist

_____

Chalkboard, Whiteboard, or Easel Pad

_____

Projects

_____

Audiovisuals

_____

Drama/Music/Dance

_____

Reviewing Questions

Prepare a question-and-answer section of a lesson plan you intend to teach. Use at least four different kinds of questions. List them below and mention what type of question each represents.

	Question	Type
1.	_____	_____
2.	_____	_____
3.	_____	_____
4.	_____	_____

Projects

Look through your teacher's manual and select three projects. Specify what point of the lesson each project reinforces.

Project   **Point of the Lesson**

1. _____   _____

2. _____   _____

3. _____   _____

Drawings

In the space below, illustrate with stick figures the following stories from Scripture: (1) Jesus walks on the water *(Matthew 14:22–33)*; (2) Jesus calms the storm *(Luke 8:22–25)*; (3) Jesus and the children *(Luke 18:15–17)*.

Notes

_____
_____
_____
_____
_____
_____
_____
_____
_____
_____
_____
_____
_____
_____

▲ *Your attitude is contagious. If you have doubts, pray before you enter the classroom and ask God for courage and wisdom.*

Prayer Response

Read 1 John 1:1-4. Then, reflect on the wisdom and insight you need as a catechist to understand the Gospel message and to choose the best techniques to bring that message to your students. Finally, place your hands on the Bible as a sign of your seeking and receiving wisdom in your role as a catechist.

In the Beginning

In the beginning was the Word, and the Word was with God, and the Word was God. He was in the beginning with God. All things came to be through him, and without him nothing came to be. Whatever came to be through him was life, and this life was the light of the human race" *(John 1:1–4).*

BIBLIOGRAPHY

Cronin, Gaynell. *Effective Teaching Methods.* Paulist Press, 60-minute video.

Dues, Greg. *Teaching Religion with Confidence and Joy.* West Mystic, CT: Twenty-Third Publications, 1988.

Gietzen, Jean Jeffrey. *Questions and Answers for Catechists.* West Mystic, CT: Twenty-Third Publications, 1991.

Hesch, John B. *A Primer for Catechists.* Mahwah, New Jersey: Paulist Press, 1988.

Lynn, David. *High School Talksheets: 50 Creative Discussions for High School Youth Groups.* Grand Rapids, Michigan: Zondervan, 1987.

_____ *Junior High Talksheets: 50 Creative Discussions for Junior High Youth Groups.* Grand Rapids, Michigan: Zondervan, 1988.

McCarty, Jim. *The Confident Catechist.* Dubuque, IA: Brown/ROA, 1990.

National Conference of Catholic Bishops. Chapter VIII and Chapter XI," *Sharing the Light of Faith.* Washington, D.C.: USCC Publications, 1979.

Olszewski, Daryl J. "Questioning the Questions," *Pace 13.* Winona, MN: St. Mary's Press, 1982.

Plum, Joan Ensor, and Plum, Paul S. *Teaching Tips For Early Childhood Education.* Huntington, IN: Our Sunday Visitor, Inc., 1992.

Reichert, Richard. *Teaching Tips For Religion Teachers Grades 1-3.* Huntington, IN: Our Sunday Visitor, Inc., 1989.

_____ *Teaching Tips For Religion Teachers Grades 4-8.* Huntington, IN: Our Sunday Visitor, Inc., 1989.

Reichert, Richard, and Westenberg, Michael. *Teaching Tips for Adolescent Catechesis.* Huntington, IN: Our Sunday Visitor, Inc., 1992.

Schippe, Cullen. *Planting, Watering, Growing: The Volunteer Catechist's Companion.* Los Angeles: Sandalprints Publishing, 1990.

Schultz, Thom and Joani. *Do It! Activity Learning in Youth Ministry.* Loveland, CO: Group Books, 1989.

Nihil Obstat
The Reverend Robert D. Lunsford, M. A.
Imprimatur
The Most Reverend Kenneth J. Povish, D. D.
Bishop of Lansing
June 24, 1993

The *Nihil Obstat* and *Imprimatur* are official declarations that a book or pamphlet is free of doctrinal or moral error. No implication is contained therein that those who have granted the *Nihil Obstat* and *Imprimatur* agree with the contents, opinions, or statements expressed.

Scripture passages are taken from *The New American Bible with Revised New Testament,* copyright © 1988 by the Confraternity of Christian Doctrine, Washington, D. C. All rights reserved.

Copyright © 1994 by the Glencoe Division of Macmillan/McGraw-Hill School Publishing Company. All rights reserved. Except as permitted under the United States Copyright Act, no part of this publication may be reproduced or distributed in any form or by any means, or stored in a database or retrieval system, without the prior written permission of the publisher.

This chapter may be ordered separately using the following ISBN number.

Send all inquiries to:
BENZIGER PUBLISHING COMPANY
15319 Chatsworth Street
P.O. Box 9609
Mission Hills, California 91346-9609

Second Edition

ISBN 0-02-651204-1

Printed in the United States of America.

1 2 3 4 5 6 7 8 9 BAW 97 96 95 94 93

Benziger

Dealing with Discipline

❧

An important asset to classroom order is the [catechist] who organizes procedures in such a fashion that the majority of students are enabled to learn. This means that the [catechist] uses carefully designed, flexible lesson plans which he or she can easily alter to accommodate unforeseen disruptions, without having to abandon chosen objectives ... A well-organized classroom also implies that the [catechist] does not allow personal emotions to obstruct the purpose of the religious process—assisting in the growth of faith, love, and mutual concern witnessed in the Christian message. To become such a [catechist] takes patience and prayer.

Mary Alice Zarella from "How to Achieve Discipline,"
The Religion Teacher's Handbook

❧

In this chapter you will:

- Develop a personal style of classroom discipline based on one of many suggestions.

- Analyze a number of discipline techniques and determine their appropriateness for various classroom settings.

- Decide the steps you will take to manage a peaceable classroom.

Second Edition

Copyright © Glencoe, Macmillan/McGraw-Hill

$\mathcal{P}$art I $\mathcal{E}$xperience

The Discipline Dilemma

When he walked into the room, they stood in awe. This new guy looked tough. Johnny whispered, "His arms are as big as my whole body." Johnny was right; this guy was a giant. He looked like he might be able to rip them apart with his bare hands. Now they would just have to play rough. The new teacher didn't stand a chance, not against this group of five-year-olds.

Watching someone as strong and self-assured as Arnold Schwarzenegger come completely unglued as a teacher in the film *Kindergarten Cop* can be very reassuring. After all, if this strong person cannot maintain classroom order, then you have a pretty good excuse yourself.

Teachers understand discipline to mean classroom order. Volunteer catechists may wonder if they will ever be able to achieve order among their students. Some catechists ignore discipline, thinking that it should not need to be a part of a noble activity such as religious education, while others follow the old dictate, "Don't smile until Christmas," hoping to intimidate their students into appropriate behavior.

Coming from the same root as the word, "disciple," meaning "to learn," discipline is associated with orderly conduct, self-control, and efficiency. It is most certainly an important aspect of religious education. The purpose of this topic is to consider how discipline problems can be prevented.

Read the following three case studies from Haim Ginott's *Teacher and Child* . For each case, answer the questions that follow. Describe what you consider would have been a better approach. Discuss your answers with another catechist.

Are You Naturally Slow?

> *"Take your seats," said the teacher to his class. But one boy remained standing in the aisle. Angrily, the teacher turned on him: "Alfred! What are you waiting for—a special invitation? Why must you always be the last one? Why does it take you forever to sit down? Are you naturally slow or is someone helping you?" Alfred winced and sat down. The teacher began reading a poem, but Alfred did not hear it. He was preoccupied with more prosaic images. He visualized his teacher dead and was totally absorbed with the funeral arrangements (p. 58).*

* How effective was the teacher's response?

_____

_____

* What would you consider a better response?

_____

_____

▲ *To exercise effective discipline the catechist must first care deeply for the students and feel comfortable with them.*

Long Division

Matt, age nine, lost his way in the middle of long division. He asked his teacher for assistance. The teacher answered: "Where were you when I explained this problem? You never listen. You always play. Now you want special attention. You are not the only one here. I can't hold special classes for you." Matt went back to his seat, but he found ways to disturb the class during the rest of the hour (p. 59).

* How effective was the teacher's response?

_____

_____

* How might you have responded differently?

_____

_____

Don't You Know Anything?

Carl, age eleven, could not open the window at school. The teacher said, "Can't you even open a window? Don't you know anything?" Carl blushed and went back to his seat, cursing under his breath (p. 66).

* Was the teacher's response an effective one? Why or why not?

_____

_____

* How might you have responded differently?

_____

_____

Learn from Your Mistakes

You no doubt found the responses of these teachers to be ineffective and confrontational. In your responses, what were some ways that you would promote justice, fairness, and peace? Listed below are Haim Ginott's comments on each of these scenarios. In what ways were your responses similar to his?

* **Ginott's comment on "Are You Naturally Slow?"**

"There is no place for cutting comments between teacher and child. They only evoke hate and revenge fantasies. The teacher could have made a simple declarative statement of his intentions: 'Alfred, I am about to read a poem.' Most children respond positively to such hints. If Alfred persisted, the teacher could have expressed his annoyance and expectation, firmly but without attack. 'Alfred, when the class is ready to begin, I find it annoying to see you still standing.'"

* **Ginott's comment on "Long Division."**

"Though busy, the teacher could have been helpful to Matt. He could have said, 'Long division is not easy to grasp. I wish I had the time to explain it to you right now. Let's schedule a time convenient to both of us.'"

Fighting Back Against Power

According to Dr. Thomas Gordon, the developer of *Parent Effectiveness Training,* parents who were forcefully disciplined as children reported developing coping mechanisms, including:

1. Resistance, defiance, rebellion, negativism.
2. Resentment, anger, hostility.
3. Aggression, retaliation, striking back.
4. Lying, hiding feelings.
5. Blaming others, tattling, cheating.
6. Dominating, bossing, bullying.
7. Needing to win, hating to lose.
8. Forming alliances, organizing against parents.
9. Submission, obedience, compliance.
10. Apple polishing, courting favor.
11. Conformity, lack of creativity, fear of trying something new, requiring prior assurance of success.
12. Withdrawing, escaping, fantasizing, regression.

"Children often misbehave when they have difficulties with an assignment. They are afraid to ask for assistance. Their experience has taught them that to request help is to risk rebuke. They would rather be punished for acting up than ridiculed for ignorance. A teacher's best antidote to misbehavior is a willingness to be helpful."

- **Ginott's comment on "Don't You Know Anything?"**

"The teacher's response was most damaging. Children are never sure about their abilities. A public attack on intelligence hits their most vulnerable spot. Virulent criticism doesn't motivate children to improve; on the contrary, it ruins their initiative. Carl's teacher could have been more helpful had he addressed himself to the situation.

"'Is that window causing trouble again?' he could have asked. Carl would have been relieved, reassured, and spurred to try harder. He would have also liked the teacher for saving him embarrassment."

YOUR STORY

Take some time to recall how classroom discipline was a part of your own learning experience. Then, write your responses to the following questions, answering the way you feel right now.

1. What is discipline?

_____

_____

2. In regard to discipline, what do you expect from your students?

_____

_____

3. What do you expect from yourself?

_____

_____

4. What problems or difficulties do you currently have with discipline in your classes?

_____

_____

_____

5. Who can you talk with about the discipline climate in your class?

_____

_____

_____

6. What other assistance would you like in regard to improving class discipline?

_____

_____

_____

Creating the Conditions for a Disciplined Classroom

Discipline is not one of the purposes of religious education, but rather, a pre-condition. Children innately need limits and guidance in order to feel secure and comfortable. In a new environment, children instinctively respond by trying to understand it, find its limits, and make it their own. They will test to see how far they can go with the person in authority. This testing process will occur whether you are strict or lenient, and you should allow the process to unfold. Until the children understand you and the way that you direct your class, you are an unknown to them. Children normally do not do well with unknowns.

Classroom management techniques are meant to help the students and catechist work together to promote the students' growth in faith. Discipline should not merely restrict; it should also free. Catechists should offer students enough structure to free them to be themselves within the context of the group. They need to know their place and feel secure within the classroom.

It is necessary for you to consider the approach you will use in regard to discipline in the classroom before you meet with your students for the first time. There are various approaches to maintaining discipline. Whatever yours is, be sure it is clearly communicated and consistent. This is necessary if you are going to have the order and attention you and—more importantly—your students need for learning to take place.

For most catechists, maintaining classroom discipline is not an automatic ability, but is, rather, a skill that takes time to develop. Note especially all of the following issues.

Know Your Students

Even though most catechists spend only limited time with their students, they should learn as much as possible about each student. There can be valid reasons for a student's misbehavior. The following are some examples that you can watch for in your students.

1. **Family problems.** Family problems can weigh heavily on a student and influence his or her behavior in the classroom. If a student is not getting attention at home, he or she may elicit attention in class by misbehaving or not paying attention.

2. **Family influence.** The family's influence is always a factor. Positive influences work in the catechist's favor, negative ones work against the classroom. If the parents show no interest in faith development for themselves or for their child, the child will often assume similar values, failing to see the importance of religious education or of paying attention in a religious education class.

3. **Well-being.** How a child feels will influence his or her behavior. Fatigue can cause listless, disinterested behavior. Children who are not sufficiently well rested or well fed will often act badly out of this lack of

The New Commandment

Saint Paul exhorted the Ephesians to live a morally good life. How do Paul's words apply to appropriate classroom behavior?

"Therefore, putting away falsehood, speak the truth, each one to his neighbor, for we are members one of another. Be angry but do not sin; do not let the sun set on your anger, and do not leave room for the devil. . . . All bitterness, fury, anger, shouting, and reveling must be removed from you, along with all malice. [And] be kind to one another, compassionate, forgiving one another as God has forgiven you in Christ" (Ephesians 4:25-32).

sleep or nourishment. Children who have been inside all day without a proper outlet for their physical energy will eventually release that energy, often in your classroom.

4. **Tired of school.** Students do not relish another "school" experience, especially if they have sat in a classroom all day. One of the challenges for catechists is to "de-school" the religious education experience for their students. This can be done most effectively through creative lesson planning.

5. **Learning problems.** Some students may have reading or other learning problems. Find out about your students' needs and provide alternative methods for conveying information, such as roleplays or art.

You do not have to solve these problems alone. Most students with persistent behavior problems in religious education also cause problems during the week for their regular school teachers. You can gain a better understanding of these students and the causes of their behavior, along with suggestions on how to cope with the problems, by contacting their regular teachers.

Mutual Respect

Mutual respect between the catechist and students is essential for good classroom discipline. Students who feel a positive regard from their teachers will feel welcome and valued. These students will be greatly motivated to follow your direction and offer you respect, knowing that you respect them. State the ground rules for your class at the first session. Try to give a good impression and set a positive tone. Keep the rules simple, and do not set too many restrictions. Base your rules on mutual respect. Allow the students to participate in establishing the rules so that they are mutually owned by all. State the rules simply and clearly, and communicate them consistently throughout the year.

Preparation for Class

Being a well-organized and prepared catechist encourages good discipline. Keep the students active and engaged. Vary the activities. Make the students responsible for what happens in class. A specific, effective lesson plan that actively engages the students' attention and participation can prevent many discipline problems before they arise.

Familiarity with Program Guidelines

While you, as a catechist, are responsible for the child's behavior in the classroom, ultimately you need to inform your program's director and the child's parents of the problem. Most parishes have established procedures for reporting problems, for contacting parents when severe problems occur, and for notifying essential personnel when unexpected problems arise.

Becoming familiar with your parish's or school's discipline guidelines and procedures before you have problems will save you a lot of time and worry if you face a difficult situation. When you know what is expected of you and understand what kind of support to expect from the program, you are free to act when a problem occurs. This nips the problems in the bud before they have a chance to mature into major issues or to influence other students' behavior.

▲ *When students are recognized positively for their skills and gifts, they learn to respect their teachers.*

Natural and Logical Consequences

Psychiatrist Rudolf Dreikurs developed principles for non-authoritarian discipline based on natural and logical consequences.

Natural consequences denote the natural results of ill-advised acts. The natural consequences of a child who runs down a slick hallway to be first out to recess is that he or she may fall and get hurt.

Logical consequences express the reality of the social order, not of the person. The logical consequence for the child who runs in the hallway is that he or she may be told to go to the end of the line. (*Logical Consequences,* Rudolf Dreikurs and Loren Grey)

What would be other examples of choices resulting in natural and logical consequences?

_____

_____

How do you feel about a discipline system based on these realities?

_____

_____

Pause a Moment . . .

- Student restlessness, inattentiveness, and forgetfulness are discipline problems that occur in almost every class session. List a few examples of what you would say or do to regain a student's attention in such a situation.

- What do you need to know about your students to deal most effectively with their discipline problems?

Ordinary Discipline Versus Persistent Problems

As a catechist, you know that there are different kinds of discipline situations. Every time a student becomes restless does not mean that he or she is bored. Everyone's attention wanders from time to time. Your students would not be normal children if they did not forget your established procedures and rules of conduct occasionally. Most of your students at one time or another will fail to live up to your expectations. How you respond to these momentary lapses will affect how you—and they—react in times of real challenge.

Positive Discipline

By occasionally reminding the students of the rules, and especially by praising them when they behave well, you can help the students develop a strong behavior pattern. They will know the rules and want to keep them. Make this type of discipline development part of your every class session.

Most children occasionally talk out of turn or misbehave in some way, especially when they are excited or involved in an energetic activity (the

Memo

List your strategy for handling a student's persistent disruption of your class. What steps would you take first, second, and third?

type that promotes effective learning and is encouraged for your class). If you correct this behavior sternly, you will confuse the students. Reminding them gently of your procedures will establish a positive pattern in their minds.

Every human being, no matter how he or she might behave in your class, wants to feel good about himself or herself. When you affirm students' positive behavior and praise them for their appropriate actions, your students—even the most inattentive ones—will feel good. The more you praise them, the more they will act appropriately. Through the use of positive reinforcement and praise, students quickly learn that positive behavior results in positive feelings.

How to Discipline

Ordinary kinds of discipline situations can become persistent problems quickly when they are not handled properly. Never allow a discipline problem to go unchecked. When you see or hear something that is not acceptable according to your guidelines, challenge it gently, firmly, and immediately. Never wait until behavior has become a problem to offer correction.

An effective way to offer correction is to:

1. Stop what you are doing and address the students directly. The students are asking for your undivided attention, so give it to them. Quietly demand that the students give you their undivided attention in return.

2. Very explicitly, inform the students of the behavior that is not appropriate. You may also ask them to tell you what the offending behavior was. (Do not force an apology. Coerced sorrow is meaningless!) Focus on their behavior and its effects, not on their personhood.

3. Explain the consequences of continued misbehavior.

4. Have the students in their own words report back to you what you have said and what the consequences will be if the behavior continues. This way, everyone demonstrates that they have heard and understood.

If the problem is anything more than a procedural violation, such as speaking without permission, go to the child and speak privately to him or her. You do not want to publicly embarrass or humiliate the student in any way. Gentle reminders of class guidelines are beneficial for all to hear. You should, of course, make your praise as public as possible.

When Discipline Fails

Unfortunately, even when you use the proper techniques, some students will not respond by correcting their behavior. Therefore, you need to determine, in advance, how you will handle such situations. Here are two suggestions:

1. As soon as you recognize that a situation is becoming a problem, report it to your director. Waiting only condones the student's misbehavior, ensures your own frustration, and encourages general student disinterest and the spread of bad behavior among other students. Never hesitate to ask for assistance. Asking for help from the program director is a sign of strength. It shows that you are aware of your limits and that you have enough confidence in yourself to ask for help when you feel that you need it.

▲ *Unlike the parent in this situation, you must first get the students' attention before you discipline.*

2. You may also need to contact the parents of the particular student. Parents presume everything is proceeding smoothly as long as they do not hear from the catechist about their child. Once they are informed about the situation, they may be able to shed light on its cause, help to devise a solution, or reinforce whatever course of action you take.

Pause a Moment . . .

- What has your program leader told you about the way you are expected to handle discipline problems?

- What help and support does your program offer you in the area of discipline?

Problem Child

Eventually most catechists have a student whose sole purpose for being in their class seems to be to put them through hell. No matter what is done, the child's behavior does not change. Finally, after consulting with the program director, the pastor, and the parents, a decision is made to remove the offending student from the class. This decision is never an easy one to make, and should never be made solely by the catechist.

Students with persistent discipline problems removed from your class are not being deprived of a religious education. Those students are not yet capable of receiving one and needs more help than you can offer in a classroom setting to become receptive. These students often need individual attention, which the catechist, as the leader of a group activity, cannot provide. The catechist is responsible for the class's needs. In this sense, the group has to take precedence over the individual.

Pause a Moment . . .

- What is your reaction to the idea of removing a student with behavior problems from your class, either temporarily or permanently?

- Make a mental list of three ground rules you will use with a new group of students to set the tone for the year. How will you explain the rules to the students? How will you get them to "own" them?

Memo

Write your definition of an assertive teacher and share it with another catechist.

Assertive Philosophy

Lee and Marlene Canter pioneered an approach to teaching using assertive discipline. Their program is based on their belief that each student has the right to:

1. Have a teacher who is in a position to, and will, help the child limit his or her inappropriate self-disruptive behavior.
2. Have a teacher who is in the position to, and will, provide the child with positive support for his or her appropriate behavior.
3. Choose how to behave and know the consequences that will follow. An assertive teacher is: "One who clearly and firmly communicates her wants and needs to her students, and is prepared to reinforce her words with appropriate actions" (*Assertive Discipline,* p. 9).

Specific Catechist Behaviors

Just as the analysis of basic issues regarding discipline can add to a catechist's effectiveness, so too can an examination of more specific considerations. The following suggestions can serve as a general rule of thumb for classroom management.

Relax Before and During Class

It is difficult to direct the activities of a group of students when you are nervous or unsure of yourself. Most catechists, especially in the first year, feel uncertain. One way to deal with this nervousness, while also establishing immediate control of the classroom, is suggested by Thomas and Rita Walters. "Always be the first person in the classroom and stand at the door as the students arrive," they write. "This provides a calming effect on the whole classroom setting. Children should not be allowed to scribble on the chalkboard, talk loudly, run, play ball, . . . at any time—especially before class." Additionally, you may wish to have "seatwork" prepared for them to do as soon as they arrive, since in all likelihood not all of the students will arrive at the same time.

Be Fair

Avoid rebuking or punishing the whole class for the offenses of a few. Sometimes a catechist resorts to punishing the whole class for the actions of a few when he or she cannot determine the offenders. However, rebuking the entire class, or mass punishment, whether for this or any other reason will leave the students feeling that they have been treated unfairly. And they are right. As a result, your relationship with them will suffer.

Maintain Perspective

Distinguish between what is important and what is not, then act accordingly. When a catechist treats every occurrence as crucial, the students will soon view all attempts at maintaining order as equally ordinary or unimportant. The students will have little regard for a catechist who blows minor problems out of proportion.

Follow Through

Never make a threat unless you are prepared to carry it out. In general, it is wise to avoid threats altogether. However, if you promise a consequence for certain disruptive behavior, make sure you carry out your promise when that behavior occurs. When catechists fail to keep their word in this regard, they lose credibility in the eyes of their students, who learn that what the catechist says is not what the catechist means.

▲ *Before each class, set aside time to relax and quietly visualize how your lesson will proceed.*

Notes

How Far Should I Go?

Many catechists ask: "How far should I go in disciplining?" or "What am I expected to put up with?" A good rule of thumb is that if you do not tolerate certain behaviors in your home, don't accept them in your classroom. If you do not allow children to sit on the table at home, don't permit them to sit on top of their desks in your classroom. If you do not allow your own children to express disrespect for you, it is appropriate that you do not let your students mock one another, challenge your integrity, or ridicule people or things that should be respected.

Avoid Angry Responses

Do not discuss a matter in anger. If you or the student is deeply angry, a reasonable discussion is unlikely. Wait until you or the student has settled down before discussing the matter. Postpone the discussion for a few moments while you gather together your teaching materials or talk to other students. In any event, do not allow your anger to persist because resentment will build and cloud your judgment.

Focus on Behavior, Not Persons

The problem you are having is with the student's behavior and the difficulty it is causing the class. The problem is not the student. Do not indict the student's character. It is okay to express how *you* feel about the student's *behavior.* Keep your feelings about the behavior separate from your feelings about the student. Maintain a loving disposition while delivering a firm, yet gentle reminder. Do not allow a personality clash or meanness to have any part in the discipline of a student. Such behavior contradicts a basic aspect of the Gospel message you are trying to teach. As mentioned earlier, correction for anything other than minor infractions should take place outside the hearing of other students.

Be Understanding, but Firm

You need compassion to understand the cause of a student's behavior. It is crucial that you be firm and consistent in your response if you expect your students to work their way free of their unacceptable behavior patterns.

Never Force an Apology

If you force an apology, it will not be real and will only deepen the resentment that prompted the undesirable conduct in the first place. Make the correction that needs to be made and go on with the class. If and when the student feels repentant, he or she will come to you and apologize or make it up to you in some way.

Never Use Ridicule

Ridicule attacks a person's sense of worth and separates an individual from the group. Ridicule is never acceptable, especially in a religious education setting. It contradicts Jesus' style of total acceptance, and it contradicts

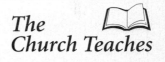

The Church Teaches

Discipline is part of the catechetical process because it can lead to inner repentance. According to the *Catechism of the Catholic Church, #1431* inner repentance is a radical reorientation of one's whole life to God, rejecting sin and evil, and feeling sorry for the wrongs we have done. Inner repentance includes the desire and the decision to change our lives, hoping for God's mercy and trusting in God's grace.

Disciplining Young Children

Even with young children (preschool grades and primary grades), a goal of the catechist should be to help the students become self-disciplining. Here are some techniques to help work at achieving that goal:

- **Model appropriate behavior** in your actions. Follow your defined classroom rules yourself.
- **Separate the students** from potentially disruptive situations. If John and Kathy are prone to talk with each other, separate them.
- **Allow natural or logical consequences** to play out. If you told the students that if they play around, then those who do not complete the art project will not have them displayed in the school or church lobby, don't display the unfinished projects.
- Allow a child's changed behavior to be the end of a disciplining situation. You may say, "John, when you refrain from calling out responses without raising your hand you may return to the class discussion."

his message of a loving community. Treat your students with the same dignity and respect that Jesus would, and expect no less of students' behavior with their peers.

Maintain Eye Contact

Do not turn your back on your class while writing on a board or easel pad. Stand close to the students, not cut off from behind a desk or in a distant corner of the room. Move about so that you are close to different students at different times and can communicate nonverbally by your physical proximity. Often, a glance, a touch on the shoulder, or physical closeness to a student will correct mischievous conduct.

Maintain a Sense of Humor

Laugh with the students, not at them. Mary Alice Zarella points out that "the ability to laugh when something funny occurs can communicate a humanity that cuts through the most difficult situation."

> *"The [catechist] who is not afraid to admit a mistake is also appreciated. And high on the list of valuable assets is the ability to see inside the most mischievous student and discover hidden virtues"* (How to Achieve Discipline, p. 72).

Be Consistent and Clear

A breakdown in classroom discipline may not be so much a matter of using the wrong approach as it is a matter of being inconsistent or unclear in addressing the problem. How can students know what is expected of them if they receive contradictory or vague messages? Clarity and, above all, consistency are absolutely necessary if classroom management is to be successful.

Consider these probable trouble areas before meeting with your students.

- How will you handle requests for use of the restroom during class time? Many catechists discourage such requests, allowing for exceptions and emergencies.

- How will you handle requests for drinks? Many catechists discourage drink requests altogether, while others include it as part of an organized break in their class session.

- How will you distribute supplies? To avoid unnecessary jostling, confusion, and shoving, most catechists either personally distribute the supplies or ask certain students to distribute them. Being chosen to pass out materials is an honor for which most students will compete.

- How will you give directions? No matter how clear you think you are or how clear you actually are, some students will not understand your directions. Determine how you will find out who does not understand. Many catechists have the students repeat back to them assignment instructions.

Pause a Moment . . .

- How do you relax prior to meeting with your students?

- Share how you might distinguish between a student's behavior and his or her character.

- What do you think is the most important consideration when developing a strategy for classroom discipline?

Managing a Peaceable Classroom

Classroom discipline that is in keeping with the Gospel message incorporates the values of justice and peace. The purpose of such discipline is to manage a classroom where nonviolence is the norm and where the catechist and students work together peacefully. Discipline that is Christian must exclude not only physical violence but emotional and psychological violence as well.

Actions in the classroom can be violent without being physical. A catechist's attitude is actually violent if it is downgrading or threatening, if he or she attacks a student's sense of self-worth, or if the catechist seeks to motivate a child with fear. A catechist can also be unjust by singling out a student unfairly, by making rash judgments, or by punishing the entire class for the offenses of a few. Such treatment does violence to each student's right to fair treatment.

Methods of discipline must be fair and compassionate. The catechist who denies justice will stunt the student's creativity. Repressive measures actually interfere with the student's right to search and to grow in faith. If discipline does not foster an atmosphere of peace and joy in the religious education classroom, another injustice occurs. Students will not have experienced something they were meant to have.

▲ *Never scold a student while he or she is in front of other students. Make behavior corrections in private.*

Contractual Discipline

Catechists teaching in the junior high or high school grades can use the **contractual way of disciplining** to foster a peaceable classroom. In this approach, the catechist and the class make a contract suggesting what they both feel is appropriate behavior. Usually there will be common sense suggestions as well as a few that are rather silly. Don't worry about the silly ones. By the time the students and catechist discuss all the suggestions and reach an agreement, there will be common ownership of the rules, everyone will know them, and the catechist will come across as "cool" and not as a parent or dictator.

> **Please Note:** *Setting class rules with the students is not the same as letting the students do whatever they want. It is a process to teach responsibility and compromise. If changes need to be made during the year, the catechist and the students can discuss that together as well.*

In developing and maintaining this kind of contractual discipline, dialogue is essential. Through dialogue, the catechist does not give up his or her authority, yet directs the religious education session so that it can attain its goal. At the same time, the students are allowed to express their ideas and opinions. In this approach, the catechist has the responsibility of reminding the students about the mutually agreed-upon rules and doing whatever is necessary to make the contract work.

The impact of such a contract for the classroom is profound. It becomes an effective model of the basic components of the Christian message—living justly and peaceably in a Christian community.

CATECHIST CHECKLIST

Lee and Marlene Canter list several positive consequences that a student may earn by engaging in appropriate behavior. Here are some of their suggestions. Which of these could you implement in your classroom setting?

- play extra music
- bring toy from home
- play games
- read special book
- work puzzles
- choose group activity
- cook
- tape record voice

- help the teacher
- type
- tutor younger children
- choose a friend to do an activity with
- assist the director
- be first in line
- correct papers

- work on special projects
- use building blocks
- work on a hobby
- monitor jobs
- teach class an assignment

Pause a Moment . . .

- Why would contractual discipline be appropriate for older students but not for younger ones?
- What are examples of emotional and psychological violence?

IMPLICATIONS

Use these exercises to apply what you have learned about classroom discipline.

Your Turn

List three of the discipline problems you have encountered. For each, suggest the approach you would want to take to deal with the problem. Also, describe what you could have done earlier in the year to prevent these problems from developing. Write your answers in the spaces provided.

Description of Problem	Reason for Student's Behavior	Your Approach	Prevention
1.			
2.			
3.			

Sample Contract

Write a sample contract for behavior that you deem appropriate for your classroom based on the age of the students you teach. (Think about how you could make this work for the early grades.) Then, interview some of your students. What suggestions do they have for appropriate behavior that can be incorporated into a behavioral contract?

Your Suggestions:

_____

_____

Students' Suggestions:

_____

_____

Draw Your Own Conclusions

Work out the following exercises as a way to help you draw your own conclusions of appropriate classroom discipline techniques.

• Describe how classroom discipline can enhance growth in faith.

_____

_____

• Describe two ways good classroom management allows the religious education process to proceed in an orderly way.

_____

_____

• Comment on how a balanced approach to classroom discipline fosters appropriate behavior for a person of faith.

_____

_____

▲ *Build a good relationship with your students from the start by having them suggest rules for classroom behavior.*

▲ *The more individual attention you give to students, the fewer discipline problems you will have with them.*

Prayer Response

Create and design a poster with a Scripture passage or other appropriate saying that can serve as a prayerful reminder of your mission to discipline in a peaceful and just manner. You may use one of the following passages or choose one of your own.

"Everyone should be quick to hear, slow to speak, slow to wrath, for a person's wrath does not accomplish the righteousness of God" (James 1:19-20).

"Whatever God does, the first outburst is always compassion" (Meister Eckhart).

"Let us strive to make the present moment beautiful" (Saint Francis de Sales).

"Whoever wishes to be first among you shall be your servant; whoever wishes to be first among you shall be your slave. Just so, the Son of Man did not come to be served but to serve and to give his life as a ransom for many" (Matthew 20:26b–28).

BIBLIOGRAPHY

Canter, Lee, and Canter, Marlene. *Assertive Discipline.* Los Angeles: Lee Canter and Associates, 1976.

Curwin, Richard L. and Mendler, Allen N. *Discipline With Dignity.* Alexandria, VA: Association for Supervision and Curriculum Development, 1988.

Dreikurs, Rudolf, M.D. and Grey, Loren, Ph.D. *Logical Consequences.* New York: Dutton, 1968.

Ginott, Haim. *Teacher and Child.* New York: Avon Paperback, 1975.

Higgins, Jo Fredell. "How to Discipline," *Growing as a Catechist.* West Mystic, CT: Twenty-Third Publications, 1981.

Sax, S., and Harmen, M. *A Peaceable Classroom.* Minneapolis: Winston Press, 1977.

Walsh, Kevin. *Discipline for Character Development: A Guide for Teachers and Parents.* Birmingham, AL: Religious Education Press, 1991.

Walters, Thomas, and Rita Walters. "Managing Student Behavior." *A Book for All Seasons.* Edited by Janaan Manternach and Carl Pfeifer. West Mystic, CT: Twenty-Third Publications, 1977.

_____ *Making a Difference: A Catechist's Guide to Successful Classroom Management.* Sheed And Ward, 1986.

Zarella, Mary Alice. "How to Achieve Discipline," *The Religion Teacher's Handbook.* Milwaukee: Hi-Time Publishers, Inc., 1978.

Nihil Obstat
The Reverend Robert D. Lunsford, M. A.

Imprimatur
The Most Reverend Kenneth J. Povish, D. D.
Bishop of Lansing
June 24, 1993

The *Nihil Obstat* and *Imprimatur* are official declarations that a book or pamphlet is free of doctrinal or moral error. No implication is contained therein that those who have granted the *Nihil Obstat* and *Imprimatur* agree with the contents, opinions, or statements expressed.

Scripture passages are taken from *The New American Bible with Revised New Testament,* copyright © 1988 by the Confraternity of Christian Doctrine, Washington, D.C. All rights reserved.

Copyright © 1994 by the Glencoe Division of Macmillan/McGraw-Hill School Publishing Company. All rights reserved. Except as permitted under the United States Copyright Act, no part of this publication may be reproduced or distributed in any form or by any means, or stored in a database or retrieval system, without the prior written permission of the publisher.

This chapter may be ordered separately using the following ISBN number.

Send all inquiries to:
BENZIGER PUBLISHING COMPANY
15319 Chatsworth Street
P.O. Box 9609
Mission Hills, California 91346-9609

Second Edition

ISBN 0-02-651206-8

Printed in the United States of America.

1 2 3 4 5 6 7 8 9   BAW   97 96 95 94 93

Benziger

Succeeding as a Catechist

*Don't mistake the material which follows as a book of answers.
Some of the following suggestions will fit your situation.
Others won't be relevant because of the unique circumstances
and characteristics of your program. You be the judge of what
is useful as you prepare for your role as a catechist.*

In this chapter you will:

- Identify and answer questions you might have before you begin a new year.

- Review the immediate preparations you need to take before teaching each class.

- Create the kind of classroom environment that encourages exciting learning.

- Develop your own personal "Catechist's Success Guide."

Second Edition

Copyright © Glencoe, Macmillan/McGraw-Hill

▲ *Mrs. Delp had learned a lot during her many years of teaching that she could offer to new teachers.*

A Catechist's Countdown

The exhilaration of Sunday's commissioning service had long since worn off—and it was only Wednesday. The cruel reality of midweek had set in for Miriam. Only three more days before she would teach her first third grade religious education class.

Her course outline that had once seemed so simple and clear, now seemed muddled. Miriam had developed basic objectives for her class with Mrs. Dalton and a team of parents and catechists, but now even these seemed too difficult to attempt.

Miriam turned to her only proven resource. "Oh, please God, are You sure about this?" she prayed.

God Provides

When Mrs. Delp called, her deep voice identified her immediately. Mrs. Delp's class was never dull; the children were treated to so much variety—from learning the Angelus to making origami figures for the Nativity scene at Christmas.

"Oh, Mrs. Delp," Miriam began, "I'm glad you called."

"Well, after being around this place for so long, they've finally given me a title," said Mrs. Delp. "Mentor teacher. That's what I am. I am your mentor teacher. What do you think?"

"I think that's wonderful," said Miriam. "But I can't teach third grade. I think I've made a terrific mistake."

Mrs. Delp laughed. "Oh, nonsense. I know how you love children. You love God, too, I presume? That's all you need to start."

A Plan

Mrs. Dalton, the DRE, had asked Ruth Delp to prepare a checklist of suggestions to help Miriam and the other new catechists begin. "As you put this 'success guide' together," Mrs. Dalton had said, "try to include the reason you have stayed so long. We're all dying to know your secret!"

Actually, Ruth realized that the key for any catechist was to communicate to the students that their parish was a place of welcome and that God loved them. Ruth often prepared over 50 children each year for First Eucharist. The next year, about half would disappear and most would not return until it was time to prepare for Confirmation in high school or even later. Nonetheless, whenever they returned, they remembered Ruth Delp. Sometimes she thought she had stayed around so long just so she could witness her former students coming back to church to be married, to have their own children baptized, to enroll them in her class.

"Miriam, I want you to ask yourself what it is you hope to accomplish as a catechist. How will you be able to observe the fruits of your labor? When will you be able to observe them?" Mrs. Delp said.

"I will, Mrs. Delp," she answered. "Just knowing that you are here for support gives me a lot of strength."

A Good Guide

Ruth knew that a catechist's success came down to the details. Always come to class more than prepared for the lesson. If the class period is scheduled for an hour, bring enough materials—you name it—to last for an hour and a half.

Yet, Ruth's query of Miriam about her love of children and God was an even greater litmus test. What she'd really like to give these new teachers was her faith. Ruth knew that the real reason she had survived for so many years was because she believed herself to be a witness to Jesus Christ. As humble as she was, she knew also that she was God's chosen messenger to these students for the time they had together. She always tried to share her love, both her love for Jesus and her love for them.

Ruth could at least think of the inspirational insert to place on the inside cover of her catechists' guide. They were the words of her favorite psalm:

> "God is our refuge and our strength, an ever-present help in distress. Therefore we fear not, though the earth be shaken and mountains plunge into the depths of the sea; Though its waters rage and foam and the mountains quake at its surging. The Lord of hosts is with us; our stronghold is the God of Jacob" (Psalm 46:2–4).

Ruth would need additional help, too. Tomorrow she would call Miriam again. Together they could work out the rest of this guide. It would have checklists and practical information galore. And it would help to get both of these ladies ready for the upcoming first day of class.

Memo

From your experience, what guidance could you offer Miriam as she prepares to teach her first class?

YOUR STORY

Whether you are a beginning catechist like Miriam or an experienced one like Ruth, you will have thoughts about what it takes to make a successful catechist. On the lines below, write your overall plan. What is it that you expect to gain from being a catechist? How will you be able to observe the results of your plan?

_____

_____

_____

_____

_____

_____

When your plan is finished, reflect on some implications of it. What will you need to do to make it successful?

Discuss your plan with another catechist.

_____

_____

_____

_____

> "Not many of you should become teachers, my brothers, for you realize that we will be judged more strictly, for we all fall short in many respects. If anyone does not fall short in speech, he is a perfect man, able to bridle his whole body also. If we put bits into the mouths of horses to make them obey us, we also guide their whole bodies. . . . In the same way the tongue is a small member and yet has great pretensions"
>
> (James 3:1-5).

Packing for the Journey

"Book One" of *Catechists in Formation* has been designed to help you gain many of the skills you need to be an effective and long lived catechist. As an "Introduction to Catechetical Methods," it is meant as a guide to your success in the religious education classroom.

This chapter offers you

- information to consider before teaching a class, whether this is your first year or your twentieth.
- a number of specific decisions you will want to make about setting up and running your classroom.

You will also be directed to other chapters when appropriate, in case you wish to revisit a particular topic in more detail.

If you were preparing for a long journey, possibly a month-long vacation to the Holy Land, you would need to make **long-range** preparations. As a catechist, you also need long-range planning. You will find guidance on your long-range needs in other chapters of *Catechists in Formation, Book One*. This chapter covers the **immediate** preparation you need to make before teaching.

The more experienced you become as a catechist, the freer you will feel to change and adapt your own preparations. Ultimately, your catechist's guide must be made your own. Where some travelers pack a large tent, cots, and sleeping bags, others are satisfied with a hammock and a blanket. While some people pack fancy cooking gear and plan exotic meals, others would rather have cheese and bread.

Pause a Moment . . .

- People pack for trips in different ways. Briefly note what you would take with you on a weekend trip. Trade your list with a fellow catechist. What does your friend take that you would also take? What wouldn't you bother to take?
- Briefly note what you think are the key things a catechist needs to succeed in the classroom. Once again trade your list with a catechist. What can you learn from each other?

Making a List, Checking It Twice

The following lists raise many of the questions that catechists ask before their first class. The list could appear overwhelming or unrealistic. To make the list a little less challenging, do the following:

1. *Note* what you think is important and why.
2. *Check* those questions for which you already have the information you feel you need. Review this information briefly.
3. *Circle* the questions that pertain to your present situation for which you need more information immediately. Note how you will get that information.
4. *Star* each of the questions for which you need to know more, but not immediately.

MY STUDENTS

_____ Who are they?
_____ How many will there be in the class?
_____ Will I have a class list ahead of time?
_____ What is the attendance procedure?
_____ What are my goals for them?
_____ Where do they live?
_____ What schools do they attend?
_____ What are their family situations?
_____ What is their history in this program?
_____ Should I expect much parental support?
_____ What is their family's involvement in the parish beyond religious instruction?
_____ What procedures am I to follow if I suspect one of my students is being abused?
_____ What do I do if one of my students gets sick?

PREPARING TO TEACH

_____ When will each student in my class have a text?
_____ When will I be able to get my teacher's manual?
_____ Are yearly grade level outcomes and lesson calendars provided?
_____ What are diocesan requirements for my grade level?

CLASSROOM ENVIRONMENT

_____ In what room will I teach?
_____ Is there anything in particular I should know about this room?
_____ When will the room be open/unlocked?
_____ What furniture will be in the room?
_____ Is the lighting adequate?
_____ Is the room too hot or too cold?
_____ Is there a chalkboard or a bulletin board I can use?
_____ Can I leave things there and expect that they will be there when I return?
_____ Who else will use the room beside me?
_____ Can I use any of the resource materials that are in the room?

PART OF A TEAM

_____ What assistance or resources can I expect from the parish?
_____ Will I have a mentor catechist?
_____ Where am I to check in before class or meet after class?
_____ Who will answer my religious education questions?
_____ Who will answer my questions concerning building and maintenance?
_____ Do I type my own letters and copy my own papers or is there a secretary available?
_____ Where do I pick up supplies such as chalk, erasers, paper, pencils, crayons, scissors, yarn, or glue?
_____ How do I arrange to use the audiovisual machines?
_____ How do I arrange to order audiovisuals?

_____ Is there a collection of resource books for catechists, children's story books, Bibles, teaching idea books?
_____ Are there resources outside of the parish that I can tap, such as a diocesan media center?

CLASSROOM ECOLOGY

_____ What type of atmosphere do I want to create in my class?
_____ Am I free to prepare my room any way I want?
_____ Will someone help me arrange the desks (or tables and chairs) as I want, or must I do that myself?
_____ Who is responsible for cleaning and straightening the room?
_____ When can I get in the room to prepare the bulletin board?
_____ Do I need to take extra measures to darken the room when I use an audiovisual?
_____ Will I need an extension cord? How long?
_____ Is there a table or cabinet I can use for supplies or display?
_____ Where will I set up my prayer corner?
_____ Where will I have my story area? What props will I need? Can I get carpet for my students to sit on?

MY FIRST LESSON PLAN

_____ Do I have any questions about how my teacher's manual works?
_____ Can I use my manual to plan lessons without further assistance?
_____ How long is each class session?
_____ How much time should I figure into my lesson plan for general announcements and gatherings?
_____ How will I know when to begin and end class?
_____ How will I introduce myself?
_____ What procedure will I use to learn my students' names and nicknames?
_____ What student seating plan will I use?
_____ How will I distribute supplies?
_____ Regarding discipline—what ground rules will I set?
_____ How will I communicate with the students' parents?
_____ What teaching methods will I use to maintain my students' interest?
_____ How will I hold students accountable for completing assignments?

MY SPIRITUAL LIFE

_____ How will I center each lesson in Jesus Christ?
_____ How much time will I set aside for personal prayer before each session?
_____ How can I include spontaneous prayer in each lesson?
_____ What can I do to show the joy I feel about my faith?
_____ How can I be a witness to the Good News about Jesus?

Notes

_____

_____

_____

_____

_____

_____

_____

_____

_____

_____

_____

_____

Getting Answers to Questions

Five-year-old children have their own unique brand of torture that they reserve for their parents. Worse than water torture, these children use "The Question."

"Mommy, when will we get there?"

"In about another 20 minutes sweetheart."

"How long is that, Mommy?"

"That's how long it takes the big hand to go from the one to the five on the clock."

"What makes the clock work?"

For the typical parent, this line of questioning quickly starts to wear thin. The sainted parent is able to maintain his or her patience for a while longer, but for most, the breaking point is near. It won't be too long before mommy tells Junior to play with his bear or count the red cars that go past.

Catechists beginning a new year, a new grade, a new book, or with a new DRE are not too unlike the five-year-old. They, too, are full of questions that need answers. However, because they are mature adults, these catechists will politely put off seeking an answer until a more convenient time.

Unfortunately, more convenient times never come. Answers concerning what to do with injured children are not received until after the child has an accident. Audiovisual requests are not made until they are too late to fill or someone else has already scheduled the machine. It is a certified corollary to Murphy's Law—"Whatever can go wrong, will"—that "You will always need the information most from the question that didn't get answered." Don't be afraid to ask any questions you may have or to keep asking those questions until they are answered.

Pause a Moment . . .

- Another corollary of Murphy's Law is "If two things can go wrong, the one that will cause the most damage will happen first." What other sayings can you add to Murphy's Law for religious education?

- One reason that questions frequently go unanswered is that there is only one program leader or DRE. Where else could you turn to receive answers to your questions? If you are an experienced catechist, how could you be a source of information to a new catechist?

And the Answer Is . . .

The answers provided here can only be general, and may not apply to your parish. However, they do offer you a starting point for understanding the importance of these questions and why you would want them answered as soon as possible.

My Students

Schedules. The most important people in the catechetical process are the students. Every catechist's primary concern is for them. It's understandable that catechists will want to know who and how many students they have before they begin the year. Schedule making is demanding and takes time. Be patient.

Attendance Procedures. Most likely you will need to turn in an attendance sheet at the end of each lesson. You may wish to have a student run the attendance to the DRE or secretary so that you don't forget and take it with you when you go home.

Using Class Lists. When you receive your class list, what will you do with it: make a seating chart? make name tags? determine small groups? form prayer teams? These are all commendable uses, but there are other things to look for in your list. Here's a suggestion:

- Get a notebook that you will use for your own records.
- Write each student's name on a separate page. Start on the front side for each student and leave the back side blank for further writing.
- Record pertinent information about each student in your book.
- Use the book to record your evaluation and thoughts about the student's progress throughout the year.

When the year is finished, you will have a complete record on every student's progress, a journal of your own progress and success, and a wellspring of information that you can use to refresh your memory when other teachers ask about these students in the future.

> **Please Note:** *These are your personal records and should not be shared directly with anyone else.*

Using Your Records Book. What information will you want to keep in your "Records Book"? The following are some suggestions.

1. Start with addresses and phone numbers of their residences. There may be more than one phone number and address based upon the family's marital situation. Usually you will receive this information with your class list. If not, ask for it.

2. What is the marital situation of the parents? first marriage? divorce and remarriage? single parent? For single-parent families it would be beneficial to know whether the second parent is dead or simply not available, because this will affect your communication with the child. You need to know the addresses and phone numbers for every parent who might need to be contacted about the student. In some cases, the students will have a guardian or other care-giver. You will want the address and phone number of the guardians of these children and their relationship with them. You should also have the name of the student's school, the phone number, and the name of a contact person there. This can help if the student is coming to your class directly from school and if you are asked by other parents to help arrange car pools.

3. Birthdates and other important times (anniversary of a parent's death as an example), number of siblings, and a list of favorite things are handy information to have. You often can learn this type of information through various "get-acquainted" exercises.

▲ *The more you know about any troubling situations your students may have at home, the better you will be able to respond to their needs.*

Notes

_____
_____
_____
_____
_____
_____
_____
_____
_____
_____
_____
_____
_____
_____

4. Use your "Records Book" to take note of students' stories, when they learn new prayers, struggles they might have with understanding a particular belief, and anything else of interest. This book is not the place to be critical or judgmental.

Contacting the Parents. Many programs ask the catechists to telephone the parents of their students before the program begins. This gives you an opportunity to introduce yourself to them, remind them of the date, place, and time for the first class, and inquire if there is any information you should know about their son or daughter. Knowing about hyperactivity, special medication, any physical or mental limitation, or unusual shyness ahead of time will help you later.

Some textbooks include letters to send home to the families. Use these regularly to involve parents in the program. To involve the larger parish community, submit student projects for display on the parish bulletin board or in articles to the parish bulletin. Check for ways that your students can be included in worship. Don't wait for an invitation, ask for one!

During the year if you plan to communicate with the parents through the students, send notes home in writing.

Preparing to Teach

As soon as you can, get a copy of your teacher's manual and student text. Study the entire book and consider the teaching instructions. If you have questions about anything, raise them with your director.

Lesson Calendar. You will also need an age-level or grade-level lesson calendar that indicates the program's schedule as well as which lesson you are to teach on each date. This will be your road map for the year. If your program does not have grade level lesson calendars, ask your DRE to help you work one out.

You will have a simple means of keeping track of where you are going and how you will get there. Use your calendar when you develop your lesson plans. Reevaluate your calendar regularly to keep on schedule.

Creating Your Own Lesson Calendar

1. Break the year into manageable parts. Count the number of class sessions and write the activities for each week on a calendar of your own that you use solely for this purpose. Include special activities such as liturgical feasts (All Saints, Epiphany) and civil holidays (Halloween, Martin Luther King, Jr.) when you will want to connect the lesson with the celebration.

2. See what chapters your teacher's manual recommends for the year. Use the ones that fit your calendar. Adjust the schedule to better meet your goals. If your diocese or parish does have an outline of suggested topics to be covered, be sure to incorporate these. Write these dates on your teaching calendar.

Classroom Environment

The location of your classroom will certainly affect you, what you can do, and how your students will respond. Establish a feeling or *climate* in your classroom of invitation. Visitors should feel welcomed and wanted. It should be bright and promote good cheer. Above all, it should be a child-centered space.

Before the program begins:

- Carefully examine the room or space assigned to your class.

- Ask when the room will be available to you each week.

- Look over the furniture assigned to you.

- Make sure there is adequate seating for the number of students in your class.

- Check that the size of your furniture corresponds to the size of your students.

- Make a list of the things that you see, what needs to be adjusted, and what needs to be changed completely.

- Try out the chalkboard, if there is one. Does it squeak and make funny noises? Where can you find chalk and erasers? If there is no board, what will you have to write on?

- Measure the bulletin boards.

- Ask who else uses this room. If your room is used by a number of different groups during the week, some of this flexibility may not be possible.

- Set up a work table for projects. Establish a place in the room (window sill, shelves, table) where you can display students' work.

- What if your class will not meet in a typical classroom at all? Some programs are designed to meet in parish halls, old convents, or in homes (often on a rotating basis). If this is so, how comfortable are you with this arrangement? What are some things you can do to develop a workable setting for instruction?

Part of a Team

Person in Charge. Every program will have someone in charge of it, whether this person is called a coordinator or a DRE. Many parishes will also have a building supervisor or a secretary on hand while the program is in session. Such an individual is available to answer any of your last-minute questions, to handle emergencies, or to care for a sick or disruptive student.

Before Class. Where do you check in before class begins? Is there a lounge or a place in the building just for catechists where you can pick up messages and duplicated items? Does the director want to meet with all the catechists after class is over? These are questions in search of answers.

Supplies. What about supplies? You will need to know if the program supplies materials for you and how you should go about requesting them. Always plan ahead so that you can request supplies a few weeks in advance of their usage date. If your program does not provide you with teaching supplies but reimburses catechists for what they purchase, save your receipts and turn them in on a monthly basis.

Audiovisuals. Audiovisuals must be a part of your lesson plan today; your students are truly a TV generation. Check your manual for suggested resources. Determine when you can preview materials and how you should order them. Is there a budgetary limit on the number of materials you can use? Ask for suggestions about using particular audiovisual materials for particular lessons and refer to your teacher's manual.

▲ *How can catechists "pull together" to make catechesis most effective for their students?*

▲ *How will you design your room to include a reading or prayer corner?*

If you decide to use an audiovisual and/or an audiovisual machine, how much in advance must you request it? Last-minute requests normally cannot be filled. A general recommendation is to order all materials and resources at least two weeks in advance. Check the audiovisuals when you receive them to make sure that you received the correct titles. Practice with the machines to make sure they work properly and that you know how to operate them correctly. If you do not know how to run a machine, make arrangements ahead of time to learn how.

Remember: *Never use a video unless you have previewed it entirely, know exactly how you will use it, know what you want to accomplish with it, know how long it plays, and have prepared the students for it.*

Many programs have a collection or library of resource books for catechists, children's story books, and Bibles. Become familiar with these resources. They provide a valuable complement to your own gifts and the resources in your text.

Classroom Ecology

Moving Furniture. How free can you be in your classroom? This is an important question because how you arrange student seating will influence how your message is received. Consider the following:

- Desks (or tables and chairs) lined in rows facing the front are for order and lecture (or video) presentation.

- Desks arranged in a circle encourage large group discussion.

- Desks scattered in groups of three encourage small group discussion and facilitate creative and cooperative projects.

- Desks pushed against the walls leave open space for class activities.

As you can see, how you arrange your classroom will affect how you teach and the focus of your teaching. Note that the first example above (straight rows) makes the teacher (or screen) the focus of attention. The other models focus attention on student involvement.

Prayer Corner. Establishing a prayer corner is easy. Simply move furniture to create the space you want. Cover a small table or box with a cloth, add an open Bible, and possibly a bowl of water and a candle, and you have created the proper atmosphere. Change the symbols to reflect the Liturgical season. Use the work of your students to decorate the space further. Some catechists also use a crucifix or a picture of Mary or one of the saints.

Story Area. If you teach younger children, you will want to create a story area. All you need is free space, a chair for you, and room for the students to sit. Many programs use carpet samples which the students take out and sit on when the story area is in use. Your program may already have these carpet squares.

As you can see, your room has the potential to become several different areas. This can add interest and help maintain the attention of your students as you move them from space to space. Measure your room, then draw it out on paper. Then design several possible layouts for your class to use.

My First Lesson Plan

In-Service. Most programs introduce new catechists to the program, to the textbook, and to the process of lesson planning. If this has not happened for you yet, seek out your program leader. Give particular attention to the layout of your teacher's manual and ask about basic steps for preparing a lesson plan. Many programs offer a beginning-of-the-year meeting or a special catechist formation class on lesson planning. Don't miss such an opportunity. It will have long-lasting value for you. See Chapter 7, **"A Process of Planning Lessons"** for more detailed information on lesson planning.

Scheduling Time. Your first lesson is unique because you really don't know how much time you will need for each of its parts. Therefore, prepare more material than you think you might need. As you move on to your second and third lessons, you will be able to estimate the amount of time needed more accurately.

When preparing for a class, you need to account for and assign time to everything that will happen during that period. If all the classes gather at the beginning or end of the session, put that in your lesson plan and assign it the appropriate number of minutes.

Student Names. Many catechists plan special activities to learn their students' names. A first step would be to find out from the students themselves which name they prefer to go by (Mike instead of Michael, Gina rather than Regina, etc.) Some begin the year with a seating chart as a memory aid. Others use name tags for the first several classes. Still others play memory games or have the students introduce each other to their classmates. It's very important to learn the names of your students by the end of the first several classes. This shows your interest in them and helps build a class identity. Check your teacher manual for suggested activities for learning students' names.

Behavior. You will want to establish your expectations for behavior at the beginning of your first class. Keep your ground rules simple and few in number, for example:

- Don't talk out of turn.
- Don't run or shout in the room.
- Do bring your Bible and text each week.
- Be considerate of others.

Write them on the blackboard or a poster ahead of time so that your students can see them as well as hear them. Consider how you will handle drinks and the use of restrooms. A simple rule used by many catechists is: "No one can say anything or leave their seat without first raising a hand and getting my permission." It takes time for students to catch on to how this rule works, but you can show them by making it into a game similar to "Simon Says." Refer to the topic **"Dealing with Discipline,"** Chapter 8 of *Catechists in Formation, Book One,* for a more detailed presentation about keeping order in the classroom.

Getting Comfortable. Both your students and you will be somewhat nervous and shy for your first class. You can get around some of your nervousness by preparing well. You can help your students get through their shyness toward you by preparing ahead of time a variety of questions for each discussion part of your lesson. Use opinion questions, personal experience questions, fact questions, and opinion survey questions as a way of getting everyone to answer at least once and hopefully several times during your first class. Refer to the topic **"Effective Teaching Techniques,"** Chapter 7 of *Catechists in Formation, Book One,* for a more detailed presentation about how to use questions to attain better student participation.

Notes

Attention Getters and Boredom

In the book, *More Than Glitter & Glue: A Classroom Guide for Volunteer Teachers*, Debbie Trafton O'Neal offers the following suggestions to get student attention:

- Turn off lights.
- Vary your volume and tone of voice.
- Play music.
- "Talk" to the students using a puppet or stuffed animal.
- Involve students in a clapping pattern, repeating after you.
- Play a game where everyone follows your instructions (Put your hands on your head. Now put one finger on your nose, and so on.)
- Use a dramatic reading or presentation.

The Church Teaches

The *Catechism of the Catholic Church*, (#2559) makes clear that when we pray it should come from the depths of a humble and contrite heart. It says that humility is the foundation of prayer and that when we humbly acknowledge that "we do not know how to pray as we ought," are we ready to receive the gift of God.

Teaching Methods. A critical consideration for your first lesson is the *frequency* with which you switch teaching methods. Remember that the attention span of your students is much shorter than your own. In your lesson plan, indicate how you will move from one teaching approach to another from time to time. It is not unusual for catechists to use six or more different activities and techniques during an hour-long class. List each of these sections of your lesson and estimate the number of minutes each will take.

Materials Needed. List ahead of time any materials you will need. Gather those materials in advance and lay them out in an orderly fashion before the students arrive. If you will be sending a note or other material home to parents, have that material ready. Be sure to explain to your students clearly the importance of bringing those materials to their parent(s) or guardian. If you plan to give your students an assignment for your next class, have it in the form of a written note which they should also show to their parents.

Homework. As for assigning homework, whether you do or not is your choice, but remember that you probably will not be seeing these students for at least a week. If you do include homework, make sure that you refer to it in the opening of your next lesson as a way to tie one session with the next.

My Spiritual Life

Sometimes forgotten in the rush to prepare for classes, making up lesson plans, and establishing discipline guidelines are the aspects of the catechist's own spiritual life. In truth, more catechists experience "burn-out" and leave the ministry because of a neglected spiritual life than have ever left because of an inability to manage a classroom. This chapter cannot even attempt to teach you how to pray, but it can offer you some suggestions for improving your prayer life.

- Set aside time each day to be with God in prayer. Start with five minutes a day and work your way up.

- Establish your own prayer space in your home. Every time you are in that spot, take a moment to pray.

- Before you begin a lesson, turn the responsibility for it over to God. Ask for the Holy Spirit's guidance as you plan and for wisdom and patience as you teach.

- Remember each of your students in prayer. Bring their needs and your thoughts about them to God.

- Participate in the prayer activities offered by your program. If none are offered for catechists, request them. There is nothing more important for you and your ability to teach.

When you are comfortable in your own prayer routine you will be able to incorporate some of your prayer ideas—including spontaneous, thankful prayer—into your lessons.

Pause a Moment . . .

- Draw a couple of possible room arrangements. For what types of activities would each arrangement be most effective?

- What are some interesting ways of learning students' names quickly?

Part III Discovery

Your First Class

Review the following suggestion as you prepare for your first class of the year:

1. Pray as you prepare. You were called to the role of catechist by the Holy Spirit. The Spirit will assist you in this role. Prayer will help you keep all the details and any anxiety you may feel in the proper perspective. Write a brief prayer that expresses your hopes.

_____

_____

2. Get the names of your students ahead of time. Determine how you will learn their names.

_____

3. Make a list of the materials you will need, such as student texts, chalk, paper, pencils, and audiovisuals.

_____

_____

_____

4. Write a few brief, simple ground rules for class behavior.

_____

_____

5. Make a diagram in the following box of how you will arrange the furniture in the classroom. Include areas for prayer and storytelling as needed.

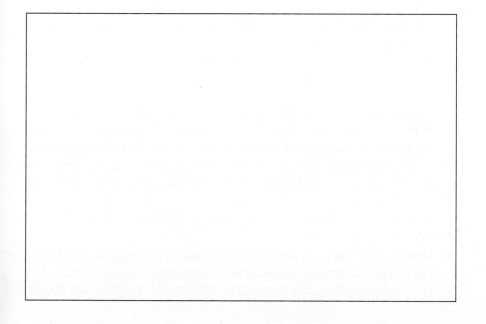

▲ *Always take time to pray before planning or teaching a lesson. Then give God thanks when the lesson is finished.*

6. **How will you establish a child-centered atmosphere in the classroom?**

_____

_____

_____

7. **What are your plans for dealing with discipline problems?**

_____

_____

_____

8. **Prepare your first lesson plan at least one week in advance.** Review it a few days later and make necessary changes. What do you need to remember to include in your planning?

_____

_____

_____

9. **Give careful thought to how you will involve all your students.** Write down the different types of questions you plan to use.

_____

_____

Pause a Moment . . .

- What other suggestions would you add to this list?
- People love stories. Develop a story that you could use to introduce yourself to your students at the first meeting. Share your story with other catechists.

Your First Class

Miriam was so nervous, she hadn't slept for more than a few hours. Why in the world would teaching 12 third graders cause her to wake up in the middle of the night? She hadn't been this nervous the night before her wedding. Well, she might not be bright-eyed for these students, but she would certainly be ready!

Nervousness and anxiety are normal human reactions to the unknown. Whether it's stage fright in front of hundreds of our peers before we make a presentation or first-night jitters in front of 12-year-olds, the expectations we have for ourselves don't change. We all want to do well; we all want to be liked; we all want to feel as if we have been successful. Even experienced pros like Ruth feel jitters again before the first class of the year.

Here is a list of things that you can do to make your first class more successful:

1. **Dress neatly.** Your appearance will set the tone for your students. If you want them to take religious education seriously, your neat appearance, effective organization, and control of the situation will promote that attitude.

2. **Arrive early.** Do this for every class. Students can never be left unsupervised. Check in with the appropriate people. Pick up your materials. Arrange the furniture in your room to suit your purpose. Have something for the students to do when they arrive.

3. **Greet the students.** Even though you may feel nervous, place yourself at the entrance to the room and greet each student with a smile and a hello. You can introduce yourself and begin learning names as your students arrive.

4. **Have introductions.** Before you begin presenting the lesson for the day, tell your students about yourself. You may wish to tell them about your family, job, and your own religious experience. Have them introduce themselves, telling about such things as the school they attend, their favorite TV program, or a favorite activity they did during the past summer.

5. **Review class procedures.** Make any program announcements requested by your program leader. Be sure your students understand the starting time and ending time of the class. Clearly explain your ground rules. If you have them listed on the chalkboard or on a poster ahead of time, you can point to each one as you explain it. Ask the students if they have any questions about any of these program and classroom procedures.

6. **Follow your lesson plan.** You may be nervous but try to get through the main parts of what you have prepared.

7. **Formally conclude your class.** Your lesson plan should include the last one or two steps of your class. Summarize the main points of the lesson. Make any necessary announcements and hand out any parent notes or student assignments. Be sure your students have gathered together their student books and other materials. Check to be sure everyone has his or her own belongings. Dismiss the students in an orderly fashion. Stand at the door as they leave, saying good-bye to each one. If students want to talk with you, ask them to wait until after the rest of the class has left.

When you finish your first class, pause a moment to give thanks to God for the gifts that you were given. Then, take a moment to review your experience, comparing it to what you had expected. Make notes on your lesson plan about how particular parts worked. Go over your student list, trying to recall as many faces as you can. Take a moment or two to look over next week's lesson and write down one or two things you want to keep in mind based on what you have learned from teaching your first class. Check to make sure that your room is left in good order and that nothing has been left behind. Spend a few minutes with your DRE or another catechist, talking about your experience. Tomorrow you begin to plan your second class.

Pause a Moment . . .

- What suggestions would you want to include on a list of things to do to prepare for your first class?

- Why would your dress and attitude establish a student's expectation of your class?

▲ *The Good News of Jesus brings its own measure of success.*

Go and Teach

You now have the tools you need to be an effective teacher and catechist. Believe in yourself, trust in God, and care for your students. May your career as a catechist be long and prosperous!

Prayer Response

Reflect on the following reading:

"You have been told, O man, what is good, and what the Lord requires of you: Only to do the right and to love goodness, and to walk humbly with your God" (Micah 6:8).

How can you, as a catechist, do what is right, love goodness, and walk humbly with God?

_____

_____

_____

_____

_____

_____

▲ *Believe in yourself, trust in God, and care for your students. They will love you for it.*

BIBLIOGRAPHY

Catechists of Our Lady of Good Counsel. "Practical Pointers and Helpful Hints for Catechists," *The Catechist*, Vol. 26, No. 1, September 1992.

Hesch, John B. *A Primer for Catechists*. Mahwah, NJ: Paulist Press, 1988.

Manternach, Janaan, and Pfeiffer, Carl J. *Creative Catechist*. West Mystic, CT: Twenty-Third Publications, 1991.

Debbie Trafton O'Neal. *More Than Glitter & Glue: A Classroom Guide for Volunteer Teachers*. Minneapolis, MN: Augsburg Fortress, 1992.

Walters, Thomas P., and Walters, Rita Tyson. *Making a Difference: A Catechist's Guide to Successful Classroom Management*. Kansas City: Sheed & Ward, 1986.

_____ *Working Smarter, Not Harder: A Survival Guide for Catechists*. Huntington, IN: Our Sunday Visitor, 1991.

Nihil Obstat
The Reverend Robert D. Lunsford, M. A.

Imprimatur
The Most Reverend Kenneth J. Povish, D. D.
Bishop of Lansing
June 24, 1993

The *Nihil Obstat* and *Imprimatur* are official declarations that a book or pamphlet is free of doctrinal or moral error. No implication is contained therein that those who have granted the *Nihil Obstat* and *Imprimatur* agree with the contents, opinions, or statements expressed.

Scripture passages are taken from *The New American Bible with Revised New Testament*, copyright © 1988 by the Confraternity of Christian Doctrine, Washington, D.C. All rights reserved.

Copyright © 1994 by the Glencoe Division of Macmillan/McGraw-Hill School Publishing Company. All rights reserved. Except as permitted under the United States Copyright Act, no part of this publication may be reproduced or distributed in any form or by any means, or stored in a database or retrieval system, without the prior written permission of the publisher.

This chapter may be ordered separately using the following ISBN number.

Send all inquiries to:
BENZIGER PUBLISHING COMPANY
15319 Chatsworth Street
P.O. Box 9609
Mission Hills, California 91346-9609

Second Edition

ISBN 0-02-651208-4

Printed in the United States of America.

1 2 3 4 5 6 7 8 9 BAW 97 96 95 94 93